ECONOMICS
OF
WORK

SECOND EDITION

H. CRAIG PETERSEN, Ph. D.

DEPARTMENT OF ECONOMICS
UTAH STATE UNIVERSITY
LOGAN, UTAH

G68
PUBLISHED BY
SOUTH-WESTERN PUBLISHING CO.
CINCINNATI   WEST CHICAGO, IL   CARROLLTON, TX   LIVERMORE, CA

ISBN: 0-538-07681-X

Library of Congress Catalog Card Number: 87-61076

2 3 4 5 6 7 8 9 K 6 5 4 3 2 1 0 9 8

Printed in the United States of America

Photo credits for chapter openers:

p. 11—Photo by Sharon Osgood
p. 26—Courtesy of the New York Stock Exchange
p. 74—© 1950, 1952 United Feature Syndicate, Inc.
p. 115—Xerox Corporation
p. 143—New York Convention & Visitors Bureau

PREFACE

Every day you are faced with choices that involve earning and spending money. Many of these decisions are confusing and difficult. By increasing your understanding of the economic system and how it operates, *Economics of Work* can assist you in making good earning and spending choices. When you have finished the reading and the learning activities, you will have a better understanding of how business decisions are made and the ways by which they can affect your individual choices. The knowledge that you gain from *Economics of Work* should also be useful in deciding whether you agree with the ideas and statements of government officials. At the very least, you should be less confused by the economic news that you hear and read.

PREVIEW OF THINGS TO COME

Part I of *Economics of Work* presents basic economic concepts. In Chapter 1 the various types of economic systems are compared. Chapter 2 considers choices that must be made by individuals and businesses. Chapter 3 introduces the idea of a market and points out the importance of money in the economic system. In Chapter 4 the role of supply and demand in determining prices is discussed. Chapter 5 describes the purpose of competition in the economic system.

Part II considers the relationship between the worker and the economic system. Chapter 6 describes different forms of business ownership. Chapter 7 discusses future job opportunities and also identifies types of income. Chapter 8 provides important information about labor unions.

Part III examines the role of the firm in the economic system. In Chapter 9, the production of goods and services is discussed. Chapter 10 considers how those goods and services are marketed to individual consumers. Chapter 11 looks at business in relation to the local community and as part of the world economic system.

Finally, Part IV considers the role of government. Chapter 12 discusses economic barometers that gauge the performance of the economic system. In Chapter 13, various activities of government are analyzed. Chapter 14 looks at taxation and examines different types of taxes.

EFFECTIVE STUDY

Economics of Work presents many new ideas. However, the text is designed to make your learning as painless as possible. At the beginning of every chapter is a list of objectives. These represent important concepts that should be understood. Throughout the chapters are "Instant Replays," which summarize important points. A good study technique is to review this material after reading the chapter. Each chapter includes a short summary. This can also be used to review the important points in the chapter.

At the end of each chapter are learning activities. These are designed to increase your understanding of the ideas in the text. Before attempting these exercises, you should carefully read and review the material in the chapter.

Craig Petersen

CONTENTS

II. The Role of the Worker in the Economic System

III. The Role of the Firm in the Economic System

The Economic System of a Society

PREVIEW

The headlines in Figure 1-1 on page 2 are fairly typical. You can expect to see stories similar to those introduced by these headlines almost any day. You will find such stories in newspapers and on your television screen. You will also hear them on radio newscasts.

These stories make a point: There is news in the way people earn and spend their money. People are affected by events in the world of business. As you prepare to enter this world, it is important that you understand how it works.

On the way toward building the knowledge you need, this chapter provides some important basics. When you have completed the reading and the learning activities, you should be able to:

- Explain what is meant by an economic system.
- Discuss the differences between free enterprise, command, and mixed economic systems.
- Explain the connection between economic and political freedoms.

ECONOMIC SYSTEMS

Individuals have to decide how to earn and use their money. Businesses must choose which things to produce and how to produce them. People in government make choices that attempt to improve opportunities for individuals and businesses. These choices must be made in every *society*. A society is all of the people and organizations in an area or country. The way a society

1

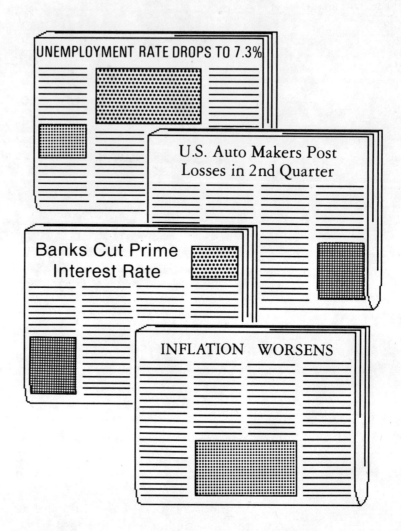

UNEMPLOYMENT RATE DROPS TO 7.3%

U.S. Auto Makers Post
Losses in 2nd Quarter

Banks Cut Prime
Interest Rate

INFLATION WORSENS

Figure 1-1 *The way
people earn and spend
money is newsworthy.*

makes these decisions is referred to as its **economic system**. The economic system includes all of the organizations, laws, traditions, beliefs, and habits that affect decision making in the society.

News stories often discuss the economy. For example, you might read that "the United States economy is the strongest in the world." Or a television newscaster might announce that "the outlook for the economy is good." The term **economy** refers to all the places in a society where earning and spending decisions are made. Two important parts of the economy are households and firms. A **household** is a small group of people who make their earning and spending decisions together. In most cases a household is the same as a family. A **firm** is just another name for a business. For example, the Ford Motor Company is a firm. All of the firms that make a particular product are referred to as an **industry**. The Ford Motor Company, General Motors Corporation, and the other car manufacturers make up the automobile industry.

A society consists of people with similar goals or interests.

The way spending and earning decisions are made in a society is referred to as the economic system of that society.

FREE ENTERPRISE SYSTEMS

The economic system of a society is determined by many factors, such as location, history, and tradition. Economic systems can be grouped into three broad categories:
- Free enterprise
- Command
- Mixed

A *free enterprise system* is one in which households and the managers of firms are free to make their own choices about earning and spending activities. Such a system is based on decentralized decision making; that is, decisions are made by individuals rather than by one person or a small group of people. There may be laws that apply to business activities. But within the limits of these laws, people are free to make their own choices. At least four important freedoms exist in a free enterprise system.

Freedom to Own Property

Private property is a requirement of a free enterprise system. To have private property means to have things that belong to you. You have the right to decide what to do with this property. Unless you violate the law, private property cannot be taken from you. Of course, other people have the same rights to their private property.

For example, suppose you buy a car with money you have earned. The car is your private property. As long as you don't break the law, you can use it any way you wish. You can drive it wherever you want, and you don't have to share the car with any other person. You can paint it the color of your choice and decorate the interior to suit your tastes.

Freedom to Buy

In a free enterprise system, spending decisions are made by individuals. No one can force you to buy things that you don't want. Unless you break the law, you have complete freedom of choice in using your money. If you have enough money, you can buy a new suit or dress. If you want to go to a concert, all that is required is that you be willing and able to buy a ticket. Similarly, you have the right to buy all the meat and fruit you can afford.

Freedom to Produce and Sell

Firms are free to produce and sell whatever products they believe people will buy. An individual can open a new gas station on the corner even though the other three corners of the intersection already have gas stations. A supermarket is free to expand and sell cameras. Managers of a movie theater can close down the business whenever they choose.

In a free enterprise system, firms can use whatever materials and methods the managers select for production. The firm can also charge whatever it wants for its product. The only restriction on price comes from buyers. If the price is set too high, then the firm will not be able to sell its product. Buyers will purchase from other firms instead.

Freedom to Work

Suppose you decide to baby-sit or do yard work. When you take a job, you are selling your time. The person who pays you is buying your time. This arrangement is an example of free enterprise. You are free to accept or refuse the work. The person who hires you is free to accept or reject your offer to do the work. An agreement is made between the worker and the employer. It exists because both parties believe that they will be better off as a result of their choices.

Illus. 1-1 *In a free enterprise system, firms are free to produce and sell whatever products they believe people will buy.*

In a free enterprise system no one can force you into a career as a ballet dancer or a teacher. Similarly, no one can prevent you from trying to succeed in some other occupation. People make their own choices. Some of these choices may prove to be wise, and some may not. But the important point is that people are free to decide for themselves.

Instant Replay

> In a free enterprise system, earning and spending decisions are decentralized; that is, they are made by individuals.
>
> Freedoms in a free enterprise system include the rights to own property, to buy, to sell and produce, and to work.

COMMAND SYSTEMS

In a *command system* the individual usually has little to say about economic decisions. In such systems the government is usually controlled by a small group of people. These people make most of the important economic decisions. They decide what and how much to produce in the economy. They select how products will be made and the prices at which they will be sold. The government decides where people will work and how much they will earn. It is difficult to change jobs without government permission. Government control often extends even to finding a place to live. People are told where and in what kind of house or apartment they will live.

Under command systems individuals *are* allowed to have certain types of private property. For example, people own their clothes and the food they buy. Some people own bicycles and a few own cars. But all of the businesses that make and sell these goods are owned by the government. Land, houses, and factories all belong to the government. The government also owns all of the oil, coal, iron, and other natural resources.

A major difference between command and free enterprise systems centers on freedom. In a command system, a great deal of power is given to a small group of people. Almost always, the result is that the individual citizens have little freedom. People are told what to make, where to work, what they can own, and how much they will pay for the things they buy. That is, decisions are centralized. In contrast, you have already learned that choices are decentralized in a free enterprise system. Individuals are free to make the decisions that they believe are best.

Illus. 1-2 *In command systems, property is owned by the government; but in a free enterprise system, individuals are the owners.*

With the power to make economic decisions, government also gains the power to control its citizens in other ways. To understand how economic power can be used for control, consider jobs and housing. Under a command system the government tells people where they can work and live. People who want good jobs and a comfortable house or apartment don't criticize the government. Those who speak out are simply not allowed to have the best jobs. They are often given poor housing. If criticism is loud enough, these people can be sent to prison.

Economic and political freedom are closely connected. Economic freedom refers to the individual's right to make her or his own earning and spending decisions. Political freedom involves being able to voice opinions, even though they may be unpopular. When economic freedom is taken away, political freedom is also

Economics of Work

reduced. The government has the power to punish those who speak out by not allowing them to have good jobs and housing. Thus, free speech can be risky.

No country in the world today has a complete command system. However, some of the nations of Eastern Europe are close to being command economies. The U.S.S.R. and East Germany are examples. Citizens of these two countries have only limited opportunities to make their own earning and spending decisions.

MIXED SYSTEMS

Life in a free enterprise system provides economic and political freedom. However, there can still be problems with such a system. Remember, choices and decisions are made by individuals. The people who make the decisions are free to consider their own best interests. Sometimes these people do not consider the needs and wants of the whole society.

For example, a company that makes paper or chemicals may decide to use the cheapest way to dispose of its wastes. It may just dump them into a nearby river. Putting the wastes in the river may be a good solution for the company, but not for society. The river will become polluted and the water unsafe. Fish in the river will be killed. The river can no longer be used for swimming. The source of drinking water for entire cities could be ruined. In a pure free enterprise system, there would be no way to stop this activity.

Clearly some controls are necessary. Individuals cannot be allowed to take actions or to exercise freedoms that hurt others. Therefore, laws are passed to control those activities of individuals and firms that harm others. For example, there are laws that prevent firms from polluting lakes and rivers. There are laws that prevent the sale of unsafe drugs and foods. The courts and the police protect people against violence.

Passing and enforcing these laws costs money. It is unlikely that people would voluntarily provide enough money to government to pay the costs of these activities. As a result, tax laws require individuals and firms to give some of their earnings to the government. These laws restrict some economic freedoms but are necessary to protect other freedoms. For example, being forced to pay taxes limits your spending opportunities, but the use of the money to pay for fire protection could save your house. Every country has such laws. As a result, no nation in the world today has a pure free enterprise system. However, the economic systems of the United States, West Germany, and Japan have many of the features of free enterprise. They are referred to as having mixed economic systems.

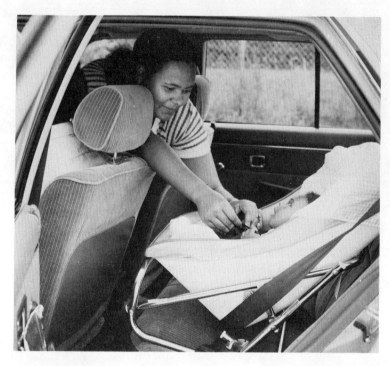

Illus. 1-3 *In a mixed economic system, the government sets automobile safety standards, such as requiring safety seats for infants.*

In a ***mixed system*** most decisions are left to individuals, but some decisions are made by government. For example, in the United States both automobile makers and the government have something to say about the cars that are sold. Automobile manufacturers can decide on style and price, while the government sets standards for automobile safety and air pollution. Of course, households finally decide whether to buy the cars. Thus, decisions about cars are a mixture of those made by individuals, business, and government.

Instant Replay

In a command system, earning and spending decisions are made by those who control the government.

Countries such as the U.S.S.R. and East Germany have command-type economic systems.

Because they limit economic freedom, command systems also can limit political freedom.

In a mixed system most decisions are left to individuals, but some are made by government.

A society is a group of people with similar goals or interests. The way spending and earning decisions are made in a society is referred to as the economic system of that society.

A free enterprise system is one in which earning and spending decisions are made by individuals. In such systems people have the freedom to own private property. They have the right to spend their money as they choose. They can make their own decisions about what to produce and how much to charge. They are free to decide which jobs to take.

In a command system one person or a small group decides what will be provided and how much it will cost. Where people will work and live is also controlled. Because economic freedom is limited in command systems, it is also possible to limit political freedom. Some countries in Eastern Europe have command-type economic systems.

A mixed system leaves most decisions to individuals. However, some decisions are made by government in order to protect society. Examples of countries with mixed economic systems are the United States, West Germany, and Japan.

BUILDING YOUR VOCABULARY

household
private property
industry
society
free enterprise system
economic system
command system
firm
economy
mixed system

In the blank space, write the term that correctly completes the sentence.

1. In a _____ decisions are centralized.

2. A _____ is another name for a business.

3. The ways by which earning and spending decisions are made is the _____ of a society.

4. People with similar goals and interests form a _____.

5. A system where decisions are made by individuals is called a _____.

6. The _____ is the place where spending and earning decisions are made.

7. A _____ is a small group of people who make their spending and earning decisions together.

8. In a _____ decisions are made by both individuals and government.

9. In a free enterprise system people own _____.

10. An _____ consists of all the firms that make a particular product.

REVIEW QUESTIONS

1. Who makes the decisions in a free enterprise system?
2. What is the difference between a firm and an industry? Give an example of each.
3. How are career choices made in a command system?
4. Name one country that has a pure free enterprise system. Explain.
5. Why are economic and political freedoms connected?
6. Suppose there were no laws that limited economic freedom. What are some of the problems a person might experience living in such a society?
7. Are there advantages to command systems?

Choices in a World of Scarcity

"Should I have cereal or eggs for breakfast?"

"Is 'B' the right answer?"

"Should I ask Tom or Mark to the dance?"

"How can I pay for the dented fender on my parents' car?"

PREVIEW

Each day, you are faced with hundreds of choices. Some involve the use of your time. There are only 24 hours each day. You must decide how many hours to sleep, how much time to devote to studying, how many television programs you are going to watch, and so forth.

Other choices deal with spending your money. Suppose that you were given $5,000 by a rich uncle. What would you do with those dollars? What part of your good fortune would be used to buy new clothes? How much would find its way to the local McDonald's? Would some of the money go to savings? How about giving $3,000 to your parents to help pay bills?

Sometimes the rules of society force people to decide between alternatives. For example, when you take a true–false test in history, only one answer can be selected. Similarly, if you are voting in a national election, you can cast your ballot for only one candidate.

Choices are a constant, if sometimes troublesome, part of everyday life. Everyone must make difficult decisions at some time. In this chapter, you learn about choices in the economic system. When you have completed the reading and the learning activities, you should be able to:

- Explain the differences between *wants* and *needs*.
- Define the terms *goods* and *services*.
- Explain what *resources* are and why they are limited.
- Define *economics* and how it relates to the problem of scarcity.
- Describe what is meant by the *opportunity cost* of making a choice.
- Identify the three basic choices that must be made in every economic system.

HUMAN WANTS ARE UNLIMITED

Have you ever been with a small child in a toy store? Do you remember the constant begging for dolls, trains, puzzles, games, baseball mitts, and other playthings? Did it seem as though the child wanted almost every toy in the store?

Teenagers and adults are only slightly different from small children. As people get older, they don't stop wanting things. People just change the things they want. You may have heard the short rhyme: "The difference between men and boys is the size of their toys." A four-year-old may want a car that he or she can push around the floor. At 12, the car must be radio-controlled. On reaching 16, only the real thing will do.

Needs vs. Wants

In making decisions, it is often useful to distinguish between **needs** and **wants**. Needs are things that you must have to continue living. Wants are desires that you could live without, but which make life more pleasant.

An example of a need is a warm place to live during a cold winter. Another need would be a coat for protection in a blizzard. The food necessary to provide energy for your body is an important need for everyone.

Many items fit into the category of wants. A new speaker for your stereo system, a fashionable pair of jeans, and a new sail board are examples.

Sometimes it is difficult to decide whether something is a need or a want. Everyone needs a place to live. But a house with a sauna and a swimming pool contains more than the basic needs for living. Similarly, everyone has to eat. But lobster and cheesecake are probably not absolutely necessary for good health. In a country like the United States, most (but not all) people are able to provide for their basic needs. As a result, most of their attention is on satisfying the wants they believe will make their lives better.

The wants of one person may be quite different from those of another. A high school student's greatest desire may be for a car. A retired person may wish to travel to far-off places. Even at the same age level the wants of different individuals can be much different. One student may save money to buy a high performance sports car. Another buys an economy car that is easy on gas. One elderly couple may see Hawaii as the vacation spot of their dreams. Another couple is happier with the excitement of the casinos in Las Vegas. The millions of products available in the economic system show the wide variety of individual wants.

Goods and Services

You don't have to spend money to satisfy all of your wants. But there are many things you can get only if you are willing to buy them. When people make purchases, they are referred to as *consumers*; that is, they are buying things that they will then use or consume.

The things that consumers buy can be divided into two categories—*goods* and *services*. Goods are objects that can be measured or weighed. Apples, books, dresses, and washing machines are all examples of goods. Services involve help that is received from other people. When you get your hair styled, the barber or beautician is providing you with a service. If you go to a rock concert, you are enjoying the services of the performers. Taking karate lessons involves buying a service from your instructor.

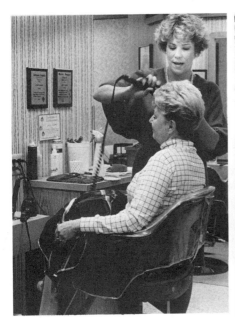

Illus. 2-1 *Consumers are people who purchase goods and services.*

Unlimited Wants

In our society, consumption leads to more consumption. A person with a new car may think about trading it in when next year's models come out. The couple who have just traveled to Spain may immediately start planning a trip to China. The child who just got a Barbie doll begins asking for Barbie clothes and Barbie furniture. People always want something they don't have. For this reason, consumer wants are said to be *unlimited*.

Instant Replay

Needs are things people must have to survive. Wants are things that make life more pleasant.

Goods are products that can be weighed or measured. Services are help received from other people.

Human wants are unlimited.

RESOURCES ARE LIMITED

Economic resources are used to produce the goods and services that people consume. The barber spends time cutting your hair. Producing electricity requires coal, oil, natural gas, or nuclear reactors. The manufacturer of a new automobile involves heavy machinery that stamps out the body parts.

The resources used to produce goods and services are usually divided into three categories:
- Human resources
- Natural resources
- Capital resources

Human Resources

Human resources are the efforts and skills that individuals can contribute to producing goods and services. The total of human resources available is measured only partly by the number of people involved. Many other factors help determine the amount of human resources available. Some of these factors are listed below.

Education. As individuals increase the amount of education they have, they also increase their personal skills. An engineering

Illus. 2-2 *Education allows people to increase their personal skills.*

student learns how to design roads and bridges. A doctor gains special knowledge useful in caring for the sick. Once these people have these special skills, they are able to contribute more to society than before.

Age.　The work that people can do changes with age. A 20-year-old can do more physical labor than a person of 70. In some countries, the number of older workers is high compared with the number of younger workers. Sometimes a war greatly reduces the number of young people available to work. At such times, it may be difficult to find enough people to do jobs that require great physical effort.

Health.　The amount of work that people can contribute is also affected by their health. In some countries, people have poor health because there is too little food. Health may also be affected by shortages of doctors or drugs. Unclean living conditions can lead to disease and poor health. Although the total number of people in a country may be large, the human resources may be limited. A small country may have people who are healthy and well educated. Thus, it may actually have more human resources than a larger country whose people receive inadequate health care and little education.

Natural Resources

All materials that come from the air, water, and earth are included in *natural resources*. Obvious examples are fuels such as oil and coal. Wood from the forests, salt from the oceans, and oxygen from the air are also in this category. Land itself is another natural resource. For example, suppose a developer wants to build a new shopping mall. A conveniently located piece of land is one of the most important resources necessary for a successful mall.

Capital Resources

The tools, the buildings, and the machinery used to produce goods or services are known as *capital resources* or *capital goods*. Capital goods are produced or purchased by businesses for their own use. Capital goods do not directly satisfy human needs and wants. Rather, they assist in producing goods or services that satisfy needs and wants.

A garden hoe is a simple example of a capital good. Few people buy hoes just because they like to have them around. A hoe does not satisfy any human wants, but it can be used to satisfy needs. The owner of the hoe can rid his or her garden of weeds. With the weeds gone, the garden will grow more carrots and potatoes. The hoe is valuable because it helps the gardener satisfy his or her need for food.

Capital goods are very important in the economic system. The electric razor that the barber uses to provide a haircut is an example of a capital good. A car driven by a salesperson and a microphone necessary for an entertainer are capital goods. So is the typewriter on which an author writes a new novel.

An economic system with many capital goods can satisfy more needs and wants than one with only human and natural resources. Imagine what a new car would cost if it had to be made without the use of machines. Today, a company like General Motors uses capital goods (machines) to form sheets of steel into the body shapes. The body parts for a new car can be stamped out in just a matter of minutes.

Agriculture is another good example of the importance of capital goods. Using modern equipment, a farmer can work hundreds of acres of land. Without such capital goods, farm families would be able to produce little more than enough to satisfy their own needs. Modern farming uses a combination of improved plants developed by scientists and increased use of capital goods. As a result, farmers produce much more food per acre of land than they could in the past. To a large extent, capital resources are responsible for the high standard of living people enjoy today.

Limited Resources

You have learned that economic resources are necessary to produce goods and services. It follows that the amount of economic resources available determines the amount of goods and services that can be produced. But only limited amounts of these resources are available in any economic system at any given time. Why are human, natural, and capital resources limited?

It has already been mentioned that age, lack of education, and poor health can reduce the supply of human resources. Even if the total supply of human resources is large, there may still be problems. For example, there may be shortages of people with particular skills. A scientist like Albert Einstein isn't born every day. In the sports world, the small number of superstars is another illustration of limited special talents. Few athletes are good enough to make the National Basketball Association (NBA). Even fewer become superstars.

Natural resources are also scarce. Hidden in the earth are fixed amounts of oil, coal, iron ore, gold, and other substances. When those fixed amounts are used up, no more will be available. Land areas for building and agriculture are also limited. There may be thousands of unused acres in the deserts of Arizona and New Mexico, but additional land for special purposes is harder to find. It may be possible to buy a plot of land in a remote spot for a few thousand dollars. But a small piece of land on Manhattan

Illus. 2-3 *In a large city land is a scarce resource.*

EPA Documerica/Dan McCoy

Island in New York City could easily be worth a million dollars. Land in Manhattan is expensive because so little land is available.

Capital resources are limited because of the sacrifice required to produce them. Many of the developing countries of the world have little in the way of capital goods. As a result, the people in these countries have a low standard of living. If such countries had more capital goods, their economic systems would be able to satisfy more human needs and wants. A basic problem these countries face is that they don't have the ability to buy or produce capital goods. Most of their resources are used to satisfy just the basic needs of the people. Such countries need more capital goods to improve the standard of living, but resources cannot be spared to buy or produce capital goods. The people in such countries are caught in an economic trap from which it is difficult to escape.

Instant Replay

Resources are used to produce goods and services.

Resources can be categorized as human, natural, and capital resources.

Resources are limited.

SCARCITY AND ECONOMICS

Economic resources are used to produce the goods and services that satisfy human wants. However, you have learned that economic resources are limited. Thus, the amounts of goods and services that can be provided are also limited. In contrast, you have also learned that people's wants are unlimited. The result is that an economic system is never able to satisfy all the wants of consumers.

When more goods or services are desired than are available, these items are said to be *scarce* Scarcity is a problem faced by every economic system. No system exists that can avoid the problem of scarcity. There will always be a conflict between wants and resources. This is a basic problem that must be dealt with in any economic system. *Economics* is a social science that attempts to understand the problem of scarcity. Economics is often defined as *the study of how to use scarce resources*.

The difficulty of living in a world of scarcity is illustrated by a story told by Abraham Lincoln. Lincoln talked of walking down a dirt road in Illinois and finding two young boys fighting. Knowing that the two boys were usually close friends, he wondered what had caused them to fight. As he came closer, he could see a single, large apple hanging from an old tree. When he was finally able to stop the fight, Lincoln learned its cause. The boys had both seen the apple at the same time and each had decided that it was his. Unable to decide who was the rightful owner of the fruit, they attempted to settle the question by force. Later, in talking to members of Congress, Lincoln observed that society faced the same problem as the boys. The problem was: Who gets the apple? As long as wants exceed society's ability to supply them, scarcity will always be a problem.

Consider some ways of dealing with scarcity. The two boys in Lincoln's story chose force as a method. Clearly, that is not a good approach. Unfortunately, some of the bloodiest wars in history have been fought to solve a scarcity problem.

Some economic systems attack the scarcity problem by limiting the sale of certain goods or services. This approach is used under the command systems in some of the countries of Eastern Europe. The government sets a maximum amount of goods such as meat, sugar, and heating oil each family can purchase. During hard times, these amounts may barely meet the basic needs of the family.

Another approach is substitution. Suppose one item is in short supply. It may be possible to deal with the scarcity problem by switching to other goods. For example, as oil becomes more scarce, substitute energy sources may be used. These other sources may include wind or solar power.

Finally, prices provide a solution to the scarcity problem. If goods are scarce, one approach is to sell them to those who want them the most. The price people will pay for an item is a measure of how much they value it. In a free enterprise system, prices are the method used to deal with scarcity. Chapter 4 covers the vital role that prices play in an economic system.

Instant Replay

All economic systems face the problem of scarcity.

Economics is the study of how to use scarce resources.

Ways to allocate scarce resources include force, rationing, substitution, and price.

Illus. 2-4 *Replanting trees is a way of conserving scarce natural resources.*

CHOICE AND OPPORTUNITY COSTS

Suppose you choose to use your allowance or wages to buy a new suit or dress. Using the money in this way may mean you have to wait before you have enough to buy something else. For example, you may have to cancel or postpone plans for an exercise bench or a new pair of skis. Each time you make a choice, there may be an alternative that cannot be selected.

The choices facing society also involve giving up alternatives. In the early 1960s, President Kennedy committed the resources of the United States to putting a man on the moon. On July 20, 1969, that dream was realized. But the total cost was over $30 billion. Americans take great pride in that accomplishment. But the huge sum of money spent on the space program could have been spent on other worthwhile projects. For example, the following projects could *all* have been paid for using that same $30 billion:

20

- Ten million dollars each to 200 small colleges.
- Seven-year scholarships of $4,000 per person, per year, to 50,000 graduating high school seniors.
- Five billion meals for hungry people around the world. .
- Building more than 1,500 miles of new highways.

How should the money have been used? Were the benefits of the space program greater than the value of the alternative uses of the money? President Kennedy decided that the moon-landing program was the best use of the resources available. The government is constantly faced with similar decisions. Current alternatives include space exploration, development of new missile systems, and construction of dams and bridges. There is a common problem in all of these decisions: Whenever resources are used in one project, they are not available for other programs.

An acronym is a word made up of the first letters of other words. Economists sometimes use the acronym TANSTAAFL to summarize the trade-off involved in choices. The acronym means *There Ain't No Such Thing As A Free Lunch.* The point is the same as with the space program example. In a world of scarcity, nothing can be free. Each time that one course of action is chosen, it is necessary to give up something else.

The alternative given up when a choice is made is called the ***opportunity cost*** of the choice. For the moon program, the opportunity cost was the education, food, and highway programs

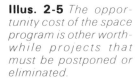

Illus. 2-5 *The opportunity cost of the space program is other worthwhile projects that must be postponed or eliminated.*

NASA

that had to be passed up. If an individual buys a new pair of shoes, the opportunity cost is the best alternative use of the money. Choices involving time also have an opportunity cost. An hour spent watching television is an hour that can't be used to study for a test. Thus, the opportunity cost of television watching is the study time that is given up.

The opportunity cost concept is a very important idea. Government officials, businesspersons, and individuals should all consider the opportunity costs of choices they make. Sometimes, choices are made without a clear understanding of opportunity costs. A good example involves wood-burning stoves. In recent years, thousands of wood stoves have been purchased by people who want to reduce their heating bills. In many cases, people with stoves believe they can cut the wood in nearby forests at no cost. Even when the cost of gasoline and a chain saw is considered, the use of a wood stove seems very cheap.

However, the true opportunity cost of heating with wood involves more than the money that must be spent. Other resource costs include the value of time spent doing the cutting, loading the stove, and cleaning the ashes. For example, suppose the same time could be spent at a wage-paying job. In that case, the true cost of heating with wood may not be so low. Even if the time would otherwise be used for recreation, there is still an opportunity cost. The satisfaction coming from recreational activities is lost in working on the wood-burning stove. Too often, individuals make poor choices because they fail to recognize the true opportunity costs of their actions.

Instant Replay

The opportunity cost of a choice is the value of the resources in their best alternative use.

The opportunity cost of time is often ignored in making choices.

THREE QUESTIONS TO BE ANSWERED

Almost all the choices that must be made in an economic system can be divided into three categories:
- What to produce
- How to produce
- For whom to produce

What to Produce

Scarcity limits the amounts and kinds of goods and services that can be produced. Think about the rare athlete who has the ability to be a professional in both basketball and football. Unfortunately, there is an overlap between the two seasons. Both sports have games in the fall. So, even though the person has the skill to play both, he is forced to make a choice between the two. That is, he is forced to decide which of the entertainment services he will provide.

What to produce questions must be answered by every business. A few companies make a wide variety of products. But most specialize in one area, such as clothing, food, equipment, or energy. Even within their areas, managers must decide which of thousands of possible products they will produce.

How to Produce

Once the managers of a business have decided what to produce, they still must determine the best way of producing it. Often, a good or service can be produced in many different ways. As an example, consider frozen meat pies. As a shopper, you learn quickly that different companies have made quite different decisions on production methods. Some pies have only a single crust, while others have two. Some brands are stuffed with beef while others require a magnifying glass to find even a trace of meat. One brand may have corn, peas, and potatoes. Another may be mostly gravy with a single pea floating in the middle.

The *how to produce* question also includes the methods used to produce the good or service. Contrast a street corner bakery and a large company providing baked goods to a grocery store. In the small bakery, pies may be made by hand. But the large firm may use capital equipment that mixes, rolls, cuts the crust, and adds filling automatically. The end results (the pies) may be quite similar. But the production methods are very different.

For Whom to Produce

Remember Lincoln's story about the two boys? Even after the apple had been "produced," there was still a problem deciding who was to have it. The same difficulty exists in every part of the economic system. Almost everyone would like to drive a new Rolls Royce. Who wouldn't like to have a two-carat diamond ring? How would it be to have your own plantation on Maui in the Hawaiian Islands? An important question that must be answered is: *For whom?* Who gets the goods and services once they are produced?

Illus. 2-6 *Goods can be produced in different ways. Business owners must decide how to produce.*

SUMMARY

Needs are things people must have to survive. Food, clothing, and shelter are examples. Wants are things that make life more pleasant. Because people always want more, it is said that their wants are unlimited.

Economic resources are used to produce the goods and services that satisfy needs and wants. Human resources are the efforts and skills of individuals. Natural resources are those substances available from the air, water, and earth. Capital goods (or capital resources) are tools such as machinery, which are used to produce other goods and services. The amounts of human, natural, and capital resources are limited.

Limited resources and unlimited wants result in scarcity. Economics is the study of how to deal with the problems of scarcity. Because of scarcity, every choice should be measured by what must be given up. In making decisons, it is important that the true opportunity cost be recognized.

Every economic system must decide what to produce, how to produce, and for whom to produce. The question *what to produce* involves choices between the thousands of goods and services that might be produced. The question *how to produce* refers to the method of producing a product. Who gets the goods and services once they are produced is the focus of the question *for whom to produce*.

BUILDING YOUR VOCABULARY

goods
economics
capital good
needs
opportunity cost
natural resources
scarcity
wants
service
human resources
consumers

In the blank space, write the term that correctly completes the sentence.

1. The _____ of going to a concert might be missing a football game on television.
2. Housing and food are examples of _____.
3. Oil and gas are _____.
4. The barber cutting your hair provides a _____.
5. _____ studies how to use scarce resources.
6. Things that make life more pleasant are _____.
7. Limited resources and unlimited wants cause _____.
8. A machine is an example of a _____ or resource.
9. _____ are things that can be weighed or measured.
10. _____ are people who buy goods and services for their own use.
11. More education increases the _____ of a society.

REVIEW QUESTIONS

1. What is the difference between needs and wants?
2. Give an example of a good and a service.
3. Think about the word *scarcity* as used in the chapter. Would a cold virus be considered a scarce resource? Why?
4. Suppose you were the manager of a radio station. What are some of the questions you would face concerning the question *what to produce?*
5. What are the three types of economic resources?
6. Give an example of a capital good.
7. What is the opportunity cost of your doing an hour of homework in the evening?
8. What is meant by the acronym TANSTAAFL? Explain.

3
Markets and Money

"The housing *market* is awful."

"The gold *market* is very strong."

"The stock *market* was down five points today."

"The farmer's *market* has a good buy on oranges."

"To *market*, to *market* to buy a fat pig,
    Home again, home again, jiggity jig."

PREVIEW

Houses, gold, stocks, oranges, and pigs have something in common. These and tens of thousands of other goods and services are bought and sold in markets. The exchanges that take place in markets usually involve the use of money.

What is money? Did you know that tobacco, cattle, beads, and beaver skins have all been used as money at different times?

In this chapter, you will learn about markets and money and their important roles in the economic system. When you have completed the reading and the learning activities, you should be able to:

• Explain what markets are and how they work.

• Describe how a market economy answers the questions of *what to produce*, *how to produce*, and *for whom to produce*.

• Explain why it is more efficient to use money in a market than to rely on barter.

• Describe the characteristics of "good" money.

• List the types of money used in the United States and explain their importance within the economic system.

THE NEED FOR MARKETS

A *market* exists when buyers and sellers come together for a *trade*. Trade is the buying and selling of goods, services, or resources. Trading in a market is based on trial and error. Sellers set a price at which they are willing to offer their goods, services, or resources. Buyers make known the price that they are willing to pay.

If sellers set their price too high, they will be unable to sell their goods, services, or resources. This causes them to lower their price in the future. On the other hand, if buyers offer too low a price, they can't get the things they want. So they increase their bids. Finally, by trial and error, buyers and sellers come to a price on which they agree, and the exchange is made.

Markets at Work

The sale of a motorcycle is a simple example of how markets work. Suppose the owner of a Harley-Davidson needs cash to go to college. An ad is placed in the local newspaper offering the cycle

Illus. 3-1 *A market exists when buyers and sellers come together to exchange goods and services.*

for sale at $2,500. Three people see the ad and come to look. Two lose interest because of the high price, and the third offers to buy but is willing to pay only $2,000.

The lack of success with the first ad tells the cycle owner that the price is probably too high. The unwillingness of the owner to sell tells the interested buyer that the offer was too low. As a result, the owner responds by reducing the price to $2,300 and the possible buyer offers $2,200. This trial-and-error process has brought them closer to an exchange. However, they must change their prices even more if the trade is to be made. If there is a price between $2,200 and $2,300 at which they can agree, the trade can be made. The cycle owner can then take the cash and go off to college. And the new owner will have her motorcycle.

There are many types of markets. Some involve only a small number of people, as with the cycle sale. Others, such as a sale at a large department store, may bring many people together. Some markets have numerous rules that buyers and sellers must follow. Others have few rules.

Buying stocks is an example of a market with many rules. Stocks are certificates of ownership in companies. Many government regulations apply to the sale of stocks. Putting a notice on the bulletin board at a laundromat is an example of a market with few rules. Some markets involve people who are in the same place. Others include buyers and sellers who are far apart. When you buy bread, the seller is in the same building. But suppose you use the telephone to place an order for a record album advertised on television. The seller may be a thousand miles away.

Whether big or small, with or without rules, local or far away, markets still serve the same purpose. They bring buyers and sellers into contact with one another to exchange goods, services, or resources.

MARKETS AND THE CIRCULAR FLOW OF INCOME

Markets can be classified as either *product markets* or *resource markets*. Product markets involve the exchange of goods and services. They bring together sellers (businesses) and buyers (households).

Resource markets exist for the trading of resources, such as labor and land. Typically, households are the sellers of resources and businesses are the buyers.

Notice that businesses and households trade roles in going from one market to the other. Businesses are the sellers in product markets, but they are the buyers in resource markets. On the other hand, households sell economic resources but buy goods and services.

Businesses offer dollars to the owners of economic resources. (For example, a worker is paid for his or her labor.) These resources are then used to produce goods and services. Money is received by households from the sale of their resources. This money is then used to purchase goods and services. The same dollars are then used by businesses to purchase more resources. These new resources are then used to produce additional goods and services. This market exchange continues between households and businesses, as shown in Figure 3-1.

Product and resource markets involve a *circular flow of income*. The circular pattern shows that households and businesses must work together within an economic system. If the exchange of goods, services, and resources breaks down at any point, the system will no longer work. If households did not sell the resources that they own, businesses would be unable to produce goods and services. On the other hand, if businesses stopped purchasing economic resources, then households would lose their source of income. Within the economic system, businesses depend on households and households depend on businesses.

Figure 3-1 *The connection between product and resource markets is shown in this circular-flow-of-income diagram.*

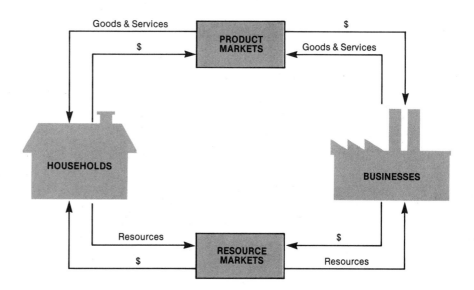

Aluminum Company of America

Illus. 3-2 *The circular flow of income is illustrated by workers who sell their labor to an aluminum manufacturer. The firm produces aluminum products which can be purchased by households with the earnings from their labor.*

Instant Replay

A market is an arrangement that brings buyers and sellers together to exchange goods, services, or resources.

Goods and services are traded in product markets. Resources such as labor are exchanged in resource markets.

There is a circular flow of income that connects product and resource markets.

MARKETS AND THE QUESTIONS WHAT, HOW, AND FOR WHOM TO PRODUCE

Chapter 2 explains that scarcity occurs because wants are unlimited and resources are limited. Scarcity results in the need to make decisions about what to produce, how to produce, and for whom to produce. These decisions must be made in every economic system. The way these questions are answered in a free enterprise system is discussed below.

What to Produce

In a free enterprise system the "dollar votes" of consumers guide decisions about what to produce. Typical decisions might center around finding answers to questions like these: Should the local movie theater show westerns or science fiction films? Should scarce oil be used to make gasoline or heating oil? Should Mercedes Benz concentrate on trucks or luxury automobiles?

Every business is free to produce what it wishes. However, households are also free to spend their incomes as they please. If businesses do not produce the products wanted by households, those goods and services will go unsold. For example, in the late 1950s Ford Motor Company introduced a car that they named the Edsel. The Edsel was probably as good a car as most of the other makes around. However, car buyers didn't like the vehicle and indicated their dislike by buying very few Edsels. The lack of consumer dollar votes that went to the Edsel soon convinced Ford that a mistake had been made, and the car was taken off the market. The introduction of the Edsel resulted in the loss of millions of dollars by Ford Motor Company.

Consumers vote in favor of a good or service by buying it. If consumer purchases are great enough, the good or service remains on the market. On the other hand, if the good or service is

Illus. 3-3 *Moviegoers vote for a film by purchasing tickets to see it.*

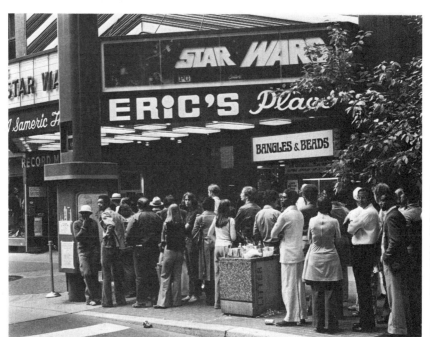

not accepted by consumers, the good or service fails. When this happens, businesses must change the good or service, or they must produce something else. To a great extent, the *what to produce* decision in a free enterprise system is made by trial and error.

How to Produce

Chapter 2 explains that some goods and services can be produced in different ways. Consider firewood for use in a fireplace. Suppose two individuals sell firewood. The first cuts the wood slowly but surely with an axe. The second has a chain saw that cuts the wood very rapidly. Which person will be able to sell the wood at the lower price? The chain saw may have cost several hundred dollars to buy. However, the worker with the saw will be able to cut much more wood each day. As a result, the person with the chain saw should be able to sell at a lower price. The axe cutter will have to buy a chain saw or be driven out of business.

The example of firewood is typical of the way in which *how to produce* decisions are made in a free enterprise system. The producer using the most efficient methods stays in business. Inefficient producers are forced out of business. They don't succeed because they cannot meet the prices of other, more efficient businesses.

For Whom to Produce

Decisions must also be made to determine who will get the goods and services that are produced. Does a new stereo go to you or to your friend down the block? Does your family get a new house or does it go to the Jones family?

Answers to these and other *for whom to produce* questions are determined mainly by income. Some people have more income than others. Basically, goods and services go to those who have the money and are willing to spend it. However much you might like to have that new stereo, it will never be yours until you have the money. Then, you must be willing to pay the price. Your parents may want the luxury home. However, the Joneses are likely to be the new owners if they can pay the price and your parents cannot.

In a free enterprise system, the *what to produce* decision is determined by the dollar votes of consumers.

The most efficient methods of production guide the choice of *how to produce*.

For whom to produce is decided by income. Goods and services go to those who have the money and are willing to pay the price.

THE IMPORTANCE OF MONEY IN A MARKET ECONOMY

Is it necessary to have money for the exchange of goods and services in a market? Of course not. Think about two 10-year-old fans trading baseball cards. One has a card that the other wants. By trial and error they attempt to find a price on which they can both agree. But that price may not be in terms of money. The trade may involve the exchange of one card for another. When goods are traded directly without the use of money, the exchange is called **barter**.

Barter is a very inefficient method for trading goods and services. The problem with bartering is that for a trade to take place, each person must have something the other wants. Often, this matching of supplies and wants does not occur. Suppose that you want a new pair of shoes and have a tennis racket that you are willing to trade. Someone else has a pair of shoes that they are willing to trade. But this person is looking for an electric drill. No trade can take place because the wants of both the barterers cannot be satisfied. To get what you want under the barter system, you would have to make a series of trades. You might, for example, trade something for the electric drill. Then you could trade the drill for the shoes you want. There might also be additional trades in between. Imagine how time-consuming and frustrating it would be to have to get the things you want in this way. Bartering is simply not a satisfactory method in modern society.

Illus. 3-4 *Children often use barter to trade baseball cards, but barter is inefficient for most exchanges.*

Although the use of money is not necessary for the trading of goods and services, it certainly makes exchanges much easier. An advantage is that everybody is willing to accept money. Money can be exchanged for the goods and services you want. If you have money and go to the owner of the shoes, you should have little trouble making the trade. The only possible problem might be in your agreeing on the price. In turn, the seller will be able to use the money directly to buy the electric drill. You no longer need to become involved in a long series of trades in order to match up wants. Because money is accepted by everybody, all you need to do is to find someone who has what you want. You know that the money you offer will be accepted.

Illus. 3-5 *Money is the oil that makes the economy work more efficiently.*

Money is sometimes referred to as the oil that makes the economy work more efficiently. Although it would be possible to rely only on barter, money greatly reduces the effort required to exchange goods and services.

THREE FUNCTIONS OF MONEY

Within an economic system, money has three main uses. The first has already been considered: money is a ***medium of exchange***; that is, money is accepted by everybody in payment for goods and services. The value of money in this use depends on how well it is accepted.

If people lose confidence in money, they may not be willing to accept it as payment for goods or services. In this case, money loses some of its usefulness in market exchanges.

For example, if prices increase too fast, people may come to believe their money will have little value in the future. As a result, they go back to the bartering of goods. This happened in Germany and Hungary after World War I. The money in those countries became worthless. Bartering became the common method of exchange. It took time for the leaders of those nations to bring prices under control. Only then was it possible to restore confidence in the use of money.

The second use of money is as a ***unit of account***. Suppose you go into a store and see a dress that has a price tag of $59.99. The price could be expressed in many ways. For example, the price could be in pounds of rice or in tickets to the Super Bowl. The exchange might also be in telephone calls to London. None of these measures would give as clear an indication of value as money would. Because money is so commonly used, everybody has a good idea of what is meant by a dollar. Prices can be expressed in terms of the number of dollars that must be paid. The dollar is the unit of account in the United States. In Mexico, the unit of account is the peso. In Russia, it is the ruble. In all countries, the basic unit of money is the unit of account for measuring prices.

A third use for money is as a **store of value**. Suppose there is nothing that you want to buy at the present time. You can keep your wealth in the form of money. Suppose that you have a small farm and produce eggs. The eggs must be sold or they will spoil. By selling your eggs for money, you have traded a good (eggs) that will become worthless if kept. You have received a good (money) that you can store until you want to make a purchase.

Instant Replay

Barter is the direct exchange of goods and services without the use of money.

Money is anything that people will accept in payment for things they sell or work they do.

Money functions as a medium of exchange, a unit of account, and a store of value.

WHAT MAKES "GOOD" MONEY?

Earlier, you learned that many different things have been used as money. Tobacco, cattle, beads, and beaver skins were given as examples. This list could also include gold, silver, wheat, spices, and hundreds of other items. The money of Rossel Island, near New Guinea in the South Pacific, is an interesting example. Natives on the island used shells as money. Different kinds of shells had various values. The shells were recognized by their colors and shapes. There may have been as many as a thousand shells with low values. But only eight or 10 had the highest values.

The natives of Rossel Island believed that the highest-valued shells had a magic or sacred content. Some were considered so sacred that they were always kept in a box and never saw the light of day. Some were used only for special purposes. For example, the natives had a custom when a chief died, that one of the inhabitants of a neighboring village would be killed and eaten.

Illus. 3-6 *Many things have been used as money, but not everything meets the four criteria for good money.*

The victim's relatives were then paid using the sacred shells as money.

Although many things have been used as money, would you expect that everything would work equally well? Would wheat be as good a form of money as silver or gold? Would shells work as well as dollar bills? There are four requirements for an item to be considered as "good" money. Good money must be:

- Available
- Divisible
- Unique
- Durable

Available

Whatever is used as money must be available for spending when it is needed. When a trade is to be made, the holder of money must be able to make the payment quickly. If the money is large, heavy, or messy, the exchange may not be possible. For example, consider an economy using wheat for money. Traders may find that the quality and amount of their money changes with seasons and weather conditions.

Divisible

It must be possible to divide money into units of different sizes. There must be small units of money for small purchases and large units for more expensive purchases. The money system must allow for purchases of gum balls as well as multi-million-dollar jet airplanes.

Unique

To keep its value, money must be scarce. Suppose every person in the United States could print his or her own paper dollars. That form of money would quickly lose its value. This is one of the problems with using shells for money. A person could become richer just by finding more shells or by changing the appearance of existing shells. To be *unique* means that the money must be in limited supply and also not easily counterfeited.

Durable

Money must remain the same over time. Suppose an economy was using fish for money. Can you imagine what would happen if the fish money was not used quickly? The same is true for wheat, tobacco, or anything else that changes its nature in a short period of time. If money is to be used as a store of value, it must be relatively unchanging.

TYPES OF MONEY

In the United States, three kinds of money are commonly used. They are:
- Coins
- Currency
- Checkbook money

Coins are simply metal money such as dimes, nickels, and quarters. *Currency* is paper money such as a $1 bill. Both of these forms of money meet the four criteria for good money. They are easy to use to make purchases (available). They can be used to make a purchase of almost any size (divisible). They do not change in use (durable). And they are scarce and difficult to counterfeit (unique).

Checkbook money is the dollars that people have in their checking accounts. When a purchase is made, a check is simply written for the amount. Checkbook money also meets the four conditions for being good money. A check can be written for any amount (divisible). It is convenient to carry a checkbook when shopping (available). The signature on a check makes it at least somewhat hard to use without permission (unique). Since each check is used only once, it is durable enough for its purpose.

When people think about money, coins and currency most often come to mind. However, about 80 percent of all payments for purchases in our economic system are made by check. Checkbook money is popular because of its advantages over coins and currency. It would be cumbersome to have enough coins and currency to buy a house. But the exchange can be made with a single check. If a large sum of cash is lost, it is much more serious than if you lose your checkbook. Also, using checks gives you a receipt when they are returned by the bank. Checks also provide an easy method for keeping track of how much you have spent.

Instant Replay

"Good" money must be available, divisible, unique, and durable.

Coins are money made of metal, and currency is paper money.

Checkbook money is the dollars that people have in their checking accounts. Most large payments are made by check.

SUMMARY

Markets exist when buyers and sellers come together to trade goods, services, and resources. In a free enterprise system, prices are determined by trial and error. Sellers and buyers change their prices until they can agree, and then the exchange is made.

There is a circular flow of income between product and resource markets. Businesses provide income to households in return for resources. Households use that income to buy goods and services. Businesses then use the money to buy additional resources, and so forth.

In a free enterprise system, the question of *what to produce* is answered by consumers. In spending their dollars, consumers "vote" for the goods they want. The most efficient methods of production determine *how to produce. For whom to produce* is determined by who has the income and how they decide to spend it.

The direct exchange of goods and services is called barter. Barter is inefficient because a trade can take place only if each party has exactly what the other wants. Money acts as an oil to the system. Because everyone wants money, it is not necessary to match wants and holdings as with barter.

Money has three functions. Money is a medium of exchange, a unit of account, and a store of value. For something to work well as money, it must be available, durable, divisible, and unique. In the United States, the three most important forms of money are coins, currency, and checkbook money. Because of its advantages, checkbook money is the most frequently used medium of exchange in making payments for purchases.

BUILDING YOUR VOCABULARY

unit of account
barter
resource markets
coins
store of value
trade
circular flow of
 income
medium of
 exchange
currency
product markets
markets
checkbook money

In the blank space, write the term that correctly completes the sentence.

1. _____ are money made of metal.

2. When money is used to add to a person's wealth, it is acting as a _____.

3. Paper money is called _____.

4. The continual movement of income between product and resource markets is the _____.

5. _____ assist in the exchange of labor and land.

6. _____ is the exchange of goods, services, and resources between individuals and firms in the economic system.

7. A _____ is something that is widely accepted in payment for goods, services, and resources.

8. As a method of expressing prices, money functions as a _____.

9. Direct exchange of goods and services is _____.

10. _____ assist in the exchange of goods and services.

11. _____ bring buyers and sellers together for trade.

12. Most large payments are made using _____.

1. Give an example of a good or service that is sold in a product market. Give an example of something sold in a resource market.
2. How do the resources owned by a household affect the amount of income that a household can earn?
3. Why are inefficient companies likely to fail in a market economy?
4. Why is barter an inefficient method for making exchanges?
5. Why must money be scarce?
6. What are some of the markets that you have participated in during the last week? Describe these markets.
7. Which are most important—product markets or resource markets?

Supply, Demand, and Prices

Darci: "Would you help me rob a bank if I promised you a million dollars?"

Dan: "For a million dollars I'd do almost anything."

Darci: "Would you do the job for $1.98?"

Dan: "Of course not! What kind of person do you think I am?"

Darci: "We've already determined that. Now we're just haggling over the price."

PREVIEW

The menu above the counter at McDonald's lists all the types of food that are available and their prices. Before placing your order, you can determine just how much of your money you will have to spend. Similarly, there is a price for each of the thousands of goods that are described in a Sears, Roebuck catalog. Prices play a very important role in the economic system by providing signals that guide consumers and businesses in using their income and resources.

In the last chapter, you learned that prices are set in a market economy by trial and error. However, forces and conditions affect the prices set by the market. In this chapter, you will learn about these forces and conditions. You will also learn about the role of prices set by the market and how prices are determined.

When you have completed the reading and the learning activities in this chapter, you should be able to:

42

- Explain how prices measure the opportunity costs of choices.
- Describe how prices act as signals to direct consumers and businesses in making decisions.
- Discuss what determines the "supply" of goods and services.
- Explain what determines the "demand" for goods and services.
- Describe how supply and demand work together to determine the market price.

THE IMPORTANCE OF PRICES

Each day, you receive signals that help with the choices you have to make. A low reading on the thermometer signals that warm clothing would be a good idea. The sound of an approaching siren signals a driver to pull over to the side of the road. The driver knows from the sound that a police car, ambulance, or fire truck is coming.

Prices also provide signals. These signals guide consumers and businesses in making decisions about goods, services, and resources. Prices measure the opportunity costs of alternative choices.

Prices and Opportunity Costs

Prices of goods, services, and resources are usually expressed in terms of money. These prices help to identify and measure the opportunity costs of our choices. Table 4-1 lists possible prices for several goods and services. Suppose that you are thinking about buying a new pair of slacks. The table indicates that slacks cost $25 per pair. What must you give up to have the slacks? For the same $25, you could buy a steak and a new cassette tape. Another alternative would be a ski pass and a movie ticket. Still another possibility would be 25 gallons of gasoline for your car.

How do you decide whether to buy the slacks, the dinner and cassette, the ski pass and movie, or the gas? Clearly, you choose the goods and services that will bring you the most satisfaction. Prices help you in this choice because they make it easier to determine the alternatives. In a barter economy without prices based on money, you would have to make guesses about opportunity costs. However, when all goods and services have prices expressed in dollars, you can quickly calculate opportunity costs.

Thus, prices help in making choices about goods or services. They also act as a bridge between goods and services and economic resources. Suppose you have a job that pays $5 per hour. The $5 wage is the price at which you are able to sell your time. With this information, you can determine how much work is required to buy an item.

Table 4-1 shows that sweaters cost $20 each. If you receive $5 per hour, you must work four hours to earn the money for a sweater. That is, the opportunity cost of a sweater is four hours of work. The prices from the table suggest that six hours of work is the opportunity cost of an electric razor. Four hours must be spent to get a ski pass, but a can of tennis balls can be earned in a little more than half an hour.

Table 4-1 *Possible prices for several goods and services are shown here.*

Prices of Goods and Services

Item	Price
Sweater	$20
Slacks	25
Movie Ticket	5
Socks	2
Record	8
Cassette Tape	10
Calculator	15
Steak Dinner	15
Ski Pass (day)	20
Tennis Balls (3)	3
Gasoline (gallon)	1
Electric Razor	30
Haircut	10

In making a decision to buy any of these goods and services, you should compare effort with satisfaction. The effort is the amount of time you must spend to earn enough to buy the item. Satisfaction is your rating of how much you will enjoy having the item. If the value of satisfaction is greater than the necessary effort, you may decide to make the purchase. This decision is made easier because all of the prices are given in terms of money.

Prices As Signals

Telephone service is a good example of how prices act as signals in a market economy. Many areas in the United States use flat-rate pricing for local telephone service. This means that a family pays a certain amount (a flat rate) for telephone service each month. Calls made within the area where the phone is located are free once the monthly charge has been paid. Long distance calls are extra.

A phone user's actions are affected by knowing that there is no charge for extra local calls. The decision to make a phone call is made just like every other decision. If the value of the call is greater than the opportunity cost, the call is made. Since the call itself is free, the only opportunity cost is the time and effort required to make the call. Because the opportunity cost is low, many relatively unimportant phone calls are made.

Some phone companies in the United States use measured-service pricing. With measured service, the basic monthly charge for phone service is lower than with a flat rate. However, phone users are charged for each local call. With measured service, the opportunity cost of a local phone call is greater than with flat-rate pricing. The time and effort necessary to make the call are still factors. In addition, the price charged by the telephone company for each call is now part of the opportunity cost.

In areas with measured service, fewer local phone calls are made than when individual calls are free. The reason is that opportunity costs are different. Each call has a cost in money as well as in time. This higher opportunity cost results in fewer calls; that is, the alternatives (the time, effort, and money) are valued more highly than the calls.

People's actions with flat-rate versus measured-service telephone pricing are a good example of how prices act as signals in the economic system. With flat-rate pricing, phone users are signaled that local phone calls are cheap (free, in fact). Because of this, many local phone calls are made. On the other hand, with measured service the higher price signals people that there is a greater opportunity cost. People consider these costs and decide to limit the use of their telephones.

Prices and the Questions What, How, and For Whom to Produce

The signals that come from prices guide the *what*, *how*, and *for whom* decisions of both individuals and businesses. Consider the *what to produce* decision. Suppose you are the manager of a copper mining company. Often, silver is found in small amounts when copper is mined. When silver prices are low, you may decide not to separate the silver from the copper. The separation cost is probably too great. So, you just forget about the silver. Now suppose the price of silver goes much higher. The higher silver prices signal that it now pays to recover the silver. This example illustrates how prices play an important role in guiding businesses in their *what to produce* decisions.

Prices also affect the choice of *how to produce*. Suppose an electric company offers you such a high salary that you decide to change jobs. You quit your job at the copper mine. At the electric company, your first big decision is how to produce electricity for your customers. Your assistants tell you that you can burn either coal or oil to produce electricity. How do you make the choice? If the generating equipment can use either fuel, the prices of coal and oil become important. If coal prices are high in comparison to oil, you are signaled that oil is the best choice. If coal is a better buy, that fuel should be chosen. In a market system, the *how to produce* decision is guided by prices. Prices determine, to a great extent, which resources will be used to produce goods and services.

Finally, prices are important in determining who gets the goods and services. Because prices measure opportunity costs, they help you to decide whether to buy a good or service or to leave it for someone else. For example, suppose you go into a car dealer and see that the price of a new Rolls Royce is $99,999.99. You are signaled strongly that a Rolls is not for you. But you get a different signal from the price scribbled on the windshield of an old Ford at a used car lot. The price range of the cars on sale signals that you have come to the right place.

Instant Replay

Prices measure the opportunity cost of purchasing goods and services.

Prices provide signals that guide consumers in deciding what to buy and guide producers in determining what to make and sell.

THE SUPPLY OF GOODS AND SERVICES

Prices play an important role in the *what*, *how*, and *for whom* decisions in an economic system. But what determines the prices of goods and services? Why does a Rolls Royce sell for as much as $100,000 whereas another car may go for less than one tenth that amount?

In a market system, prices are determined by supply and demand. Although supply and demand are related, each has its own characteristics.

Supply Curves

Supply refers to the amount, or quantity, of a good or service that businesses will provide at different prices. Table 4-2 contains supply information for gasoline. At each price, the table shows how many gallons of gasoline oil companies will provide. For example, at a price of $1.20 per gallon, 10 million gallons of gasoline will be supplied each year. If the price goes up to $1.40, 14 million gallons per year will be provided.

Table 4-2 *This table shows how many gallons of gasoline will be supplied at various prices.*

Supply of Gasoline

Price of Gasoline	Gallons of Gasoline Supplied Per Year
$1.00	5 million
1.20	10 million
1.40	14 million
1.60	17 million
1.80	19 million
2.00	20 million

Sometimes information is easier to understand when it is presented in a graph. Figure 4-1 is a graph of the numbers in Table 4-2. Notice that the amount of oil provided is measured along the bottom of the graph. The price of oil is measured up the side of the graph. The line marked with an "S" at each end is called a ***supply curve***. It was drawn by using the information from Table 4-2. For example, the table shows that, at $1 per gallon, 5 million gallons of gasoline will be produced. To enter this information on the graph, go up the side until you come to a price of $1. Then go out along the bottom line to 5 million gallons. That point on the graph gives the same information as the first row in the table. The other points on the graph are placed using the same method. Note that there are six points on the graph. These correspond to the six lines of numbers in Table 4-2.

Figure 4-1 *Graph showing the supply curve for gasoline. This corresponds to Table 4-2.*

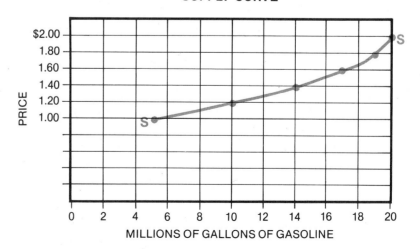

SUPPLY CURVE

Once the points are located on the graph, the supply curve is drawn with a line connecting the six points. Take a moment now to compare the information in Table 4-2 and Figure 4-1. The graph, in effect, is a picture presenting the same information as the numbers in the table. Graphs are an important tool for economists. They are used to present many types of economic information.

The Law of Supply

The supply curve in Figure 4-1 goes up as you look from left to right. Such a curve is said to be *upward-sloping*. What does it mean for the supply curve to be upward-sloping? Look at the points on that supply curve. Notice that they show that producers will provide more gasoline at higher prices. A price of $1.20 per gallon results in a supply of 10 million gallons of gas. At a price of $1.40, 14 million gallons will be produced.

The supply curve in Figure 4-1 illustrates a very important idea in economics—the *law of supply*. The law of supply states that businesses will produce more of a good or service at higher prices than they will at lower prices. It is possible that someone could find a situation where the law of supply is not true. Such cases, however, are not important for this discussion. You can assume that the law of supply is a true statement: Businesses produce more of a good or service as prices increase.

Why Are Supply Curves Upward-Sloping?   It costs money for a company to provide an extra gallon of gasoline to consumers. This cost includes buying crude oil, refining the oil, and then delivering the finished product to service stations. The cost of one more unit is referred to as the *marginal cost* of that good or service.

A big part of understanding economics is learning the vocabulary. In studying economics, the word *marginal* can be thought of as meaning extra. Thus, the marginal cost is the cost of supplying one extra unit of a good or service.

How should the managers of a major oil company decide whether to supply more gasoline? The answer depends on the selling price in comparison to the marginal cost. Suppose the managers believe that they can sell each extra gallon for more than the marginal cost of producing and supplying it. In this case, they are better off if they supply the extra gallon. On the other hand, the price of gasoline might be less than the marginal cost. If so, the company is better off by not increasing production.

The decision about increasing supplies of gasoline follows a basic rule. The rule is that production should be increased if the expected selling price is greater than the marginal cost per unit. If the selling price is less than the marginal cost, an extra unit should not be supplied.

With gasoline as an example, it is easy to see why the supply curve slopes upward. Think about what an oil company has to do to provide more gas. The first need would be to get more oil. Suppose that all of a company's oil comes from wells drilled in the United States. To get more oil, the company will have to drill more wells. This can be a problem: Most of the easy-to-get oil in the United States is already being pumped. Getting more oil might mean drilling wells into the ocean floor or working in Alaska in temperatures of −80°. Any oil that comes from these areas will cost much more than oil pumped from the plains of Texas.

In terms of the vocabulary of economics, the marginal cost of new oil would be higher than the cost of existing oil. Because the marginal cost of supplying this oil is greater, the firm will supply it only if the managers expect that the price will be higher. Remember the rule—supply only if price is greater than marginal cost.

The higher marginal cost of getting extra oil explains the upward-sloping supply curve for gasoline. In this example, the cost of oil is a big part of the cost of gasoline. So, more gasoline will be provided only if the selling price is higher than the marginal cost.

Illus. 4-1 *It is more expensive to take oil from the ocean floor than to pump it from under the plains of Texas.*

AMOCO Corporation

The supply curves for other goods and services slope upward for the same reason as the gasoline supply curve. As companies try to produce more of a good or service, the marginal cost increases. Thus, businesses will supply more only if the price also increases. Increasing marginal costs are the explanation behind the law of supply.

Instant Replay

Supply refers to the quantity of a product that will be offered for sale at different prices.

The law of supply states that more will be offered for sale at higher prices than at lower prices; that is, the supply curve is upward sloping.

The supply curve is upward sloping because, for most products, the marginal cost of producing increases as output increases.

THE DEMAND FOR GOODS AND SERVICES

Companies must decide how much of a good or service they will produce. But this is only half the decision. Consumers must also make choices about how much they will buy.

The Demand Curve

Demand refers to the amount of a good or service that consumers will buy at different prices. *Demand*, as the word is used in the study of economics, does not mean the same as *want*. You may want a new coat but not be willing or able to buy the coat. Wants involve desires and not necessarily action. Demand, on the other hand, requires action. A demand for a new coat exists only if a person is willing and able to make the purchase.

Table 4-3 shows demand information for gasoline. At each price, the table indicates how many gallons per year consumers will buy. For example, if the price is $1 per gallon, the demand is 17 million gallons per year. If the price goes up to $1.20, consumers will purchase 16 million gallons each year.

Table 4-3 *This table indicates the number of gallons of gasoline consumers will buy at each price.*

Demand for Gasoline

Price of Gasoline	Gallons of Gasoline Demanded Per Year
$1.00	17 million
1.20	16 million
1.40	14 million
1.60	11 million
1.80	7 million
2.00	2 million

Figure 4-2 is a graph of the information in Table 4-3. The curve marked with a "D" on each end is referred to as a *demand curve*. It was constructed in the same way as the supply curve. The six points on the demand curve correspond to the six rows of numbers in Table 4-3.

The Law of Demand

The demand curve of Figure 4-2 goes down as you read from left to right. Such a curve is *downward-sloping*. A downward-sloping curve indicates that when price goes up, the demand for gasoline decreases. For example, at $1.80 per gallon, the demand is for 7 million gallons per year. When the price increases to $2.00 per gallon, the annual demand drops to 2 million gallons.

The demand curve shown in Figure 4-2 illustrates the *law of demand*. The law of demand says that consumers buy less of a good or service as prices increase. Sales are greater at lower prices. This is one of the most important ideas in economics.

Figure 4-2 *Graph showing the demand curve for gasoline. It corresponds to Table 4-3.*

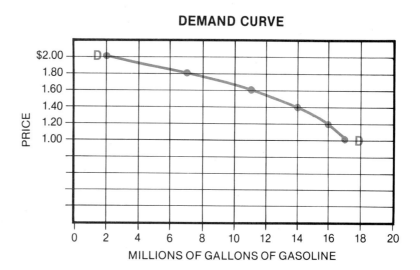

DEMAND CURVE

PRICE

MILLIONS OF GALLONS OF GASOLINE

Illus. 4-2 *The law of demand states that lower prices cause consumers to buy more goods and services.*

Why Are Demand Curves Downward-Sloping?

Think about what would happen if the price of gasoline were to jump from $1 to $2 per gallon. Why would people use less gas? One reason would be because, at the higher price, people are unable to buy as much as they did before. Remember, demand is a measure of people's ability to buy goods and services. At higher prices, the same amount of money buys less. At $1 per gallon, a $20 bill buys 20 gallons of gas. At $2 a gallon, only 10 gallons can be purchased. The first reason for downward-sloping demand curves is that people are unable to buy as much as they could at lower prices.

There is a second reason why demand curves are downward-sloping. Remember how a person's decision to buy a particular good or service is made? The consumer compares the item with other things that could be bought for the same price. A purchase is made only if nothing else would provide as much satisfaction for the price.

Suppose you are thinking about buying one more gallon of gasoline. You have to choose between that extra gallon and other items available for the same money. For example, the gasoline should be worth more than the doughnuts you could buy for the same money. Now suppose that the price of gasoline goes up by 25 cents per gallon. At the higher price, you now decide the snack is the better purchase and don't buy the gas.

As the price of a good or service increases, the opportunity cost of buying it also increases. As a result, people are more likely to use their money to buy something else. This switching to other goods and services is the second reason that demand curves slope downward.

Elastic and Inelastic Demand

Demand for a good or service can be categorized as elastic or inelastic. Demand is said to be *elastic* if a small change in price results in a large change in quantity demanded. Demand tends to be elastic if there are good substitutes for a product. For example, lemon-flavored soft drinks are much alike. Thus, if the price of 7-Up were to increase by 25 cents per can, many people would switch from 7-Up to Sprite. Hence, there would be a large decrease in sales of 7-Up.

Demand is said to be *inelastic* if even a large change in price results in only a small change in quantity demanded. Products for which there are few good substitutes tend to have inelastic demand. For example, the demand for appendectomies would be inelastic. Faced with the great pain of an infected appendix, few people would decide not to have the operation because the price was too high.

Instant Replay

The law of demand states that more of a good or service is demanded at lower prices than at higher prices.

The demand curve shows the relationship between the price of a product and the amount that consumers will want to buy at that price.

Inelastic demand means that price changes have little effect on quantity demanded. If demand is elastic, even small price changes can have a significant effect on quantity demanded.

SUPPLY, DEMAND, AND THE MARKET PRICE

Understanding the economic system involves a lot more than just learning about supply and demand. But supply and demand *are* very important ideas; they work together to determine prices of goods and services in a market economy.

Table 4-4 shows the supply and demand for gasoline at different prices. For example, suppose the price is $1 per gallon. At that price, supplies will be 5 million gallons and the demand level will be 17 million gallons. Because more gasoline is demanded than is supplied at that level, there is said to be an **excess demand** for gasoline.

What happens when there is excess demand for a good or service? At $1 per gallon, more gasoline is demanded than is available. So, some people are unable to get as much gasoline as they are willing to purchase. To get more gasoline, some of these people will pay a higher price. Suppose the price of gasoline goes up to $1.20 per gallon. At this higher price, some consumers decide to use less gasoline. Table 4-4 shows that, at $1.20 per gallon, demand drops to 16 million gallons.

Consumers are not the only ones who change their behavior when prices rise. Table 4-4 shows that oil companies will increase their supply of gasoline to 10 million gallons at $1.20. However, even at this higher price, there is still an excess demand for gasoline. The demand is 16 million gallons, and the supply is only 10 million gallons.

Table 4-4 *This table gives the supply and demand figures for gasoline at different prices.*

Supply of and Demand for Gasoline

Price of Gasoline	Gallons of Gasoline Supplied Per Year	Gallons of Gasoline Demanded Per Year
$1.00	5 million	17 million
1.20	10 million	16 million
1.40	14 million	14 million
1.60	17 million	11 million
1.80	19 million	7 million
2.00	20 million	2 million

Any time there is excess demand, some consumers who need more of the good or service will bid up the price. Suppose these consumers bid up the price of gasoline to $1.40 per gallon. At this higher price, demand drops and supply increases. Table 4-4 indicates that demand decreases by 2 million gallons and supply increases by 4 million gallons as price goes from $1.20 to $1.40 per gallon.

Note that, at a price of $1.40, both the demand for and the supply of gasoline are 14 million gallons. No longer is there excess demand. Supply and demand are exactly equal at $1.40 per gallon. Consumer demands equal the supply that companies are willing to provide.

Courtesy Texaco Inc. & American Petroleum Institute Photographic & Film Services

Illus. 4-3 *When more gasoline is demanded than is supplied, there is said to be an excess demand for gasoline.*

Because supply and demand are equal at $1.40 per gallon, there are no consumers who want to bid up the price. Since the price remains unchanged, there is no reason for oil companies to change the amount they supply. A price of $1.40 per gallon brings supply and demand into balance. Because that price was determined by trial and error in a market, it is called the **market price**.

What happens if the price of gasoline is higher than the market price? For example, suppose the price is $1.60 per gallon. At that price, the supply is 17 million gallons and the demand is only 11 million gallons. Because supply is greater than demand, there is an **excess supply** of gasoline.

At $1.60 per gallon, the oil companies can't sell all the gas that they produce. What should they do? Selling gas at a lower price is better than not selling it at all. Thus, the firms will offer gasoline to consumers at a lower price. Suppose the companies reduce the price of gas to $1.40 per gallon. At this reduced price, consumers are willing to buy more gasoline. Table 4-4 shows that they will increase their purchases to 14 million gallons.

When the price of gas drops to $1.40, the oil companies rethink their decisions about how much gas to supply in the future. When the price was $1.60, they provided 16 million gallons. At the lower price of $1.40 per gallon, they cut back their future supply to only 14 million gallons. Thus, supply and demand are now equal at a price of $1.40. By trial and error, the market price has again been determined.

Let's review how the market price is determined. When the price is above the market price, there is an excess supply. As a result, the price is bid down until demand and supply are equal. On the other hand, if the price is below the market price, then there is excess demand. Now prices are bid up until supply and demand are again in balance. Once the amount supplied is equal to the amount demanded, there are no more forces causing the price to change. Unless consumers change their demand decisions or businesses change their supply choices, the price will stay the same.

So far, Table 4-4 has been used to show how prices are set in a market. However, the market price can also be determined using the supply and demand curves. Figure 4-3 puts the supply and demand curves for gasoline together. Notice that the two curves cross at 14 million gallons. Notice also that $1.40 is the price at which the two curves cross. Thus, $1.40 per gallon is the price that causes demand and supply to be equal. That is, $1.40 is the market price of gasoline.

Using supply and demand curves, it is easy to figure out the market price. First, find the point where the two curves cross. Then read the price from the scale on the left side of the graph. This amount is the market price. Similarly, the amount supplied and demanded is read from the scale on the bottom of the graph.

Looking at Figure 4-3, you can see that any price above the market price will result in excess supply; that is, the supply curve is to the right of the demand curve. Similarly, any price below the market price causes excess demand. Demand and supply are only in balance where the curves cross—at the market price.

Instant Replay

Excess demand means the quantity demanded exceeds the quantity supplied. As a result, the price will rise.

Excess supply means that the quantity supplied exceeds the quantity demanded. As a result, the price will fall.

The market price is determined where quantity supplied equals quantity demanded.

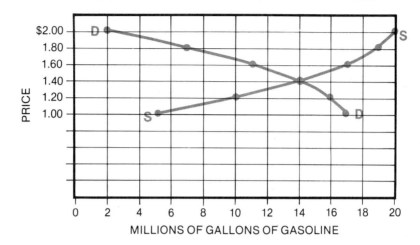

SUPPLY AND DEMAND CURVES TOGETHER

Figure 4-3 *Together, supply and demand determine the market price.*

SUMMARY

Prices measure the opportunity costs of consumer choices. As the price of a good or service increases, the opportunity cost of buying it also increases. Prices act as signals that guide individuals in purchasing decisions. Businesses are guided by prices in their choices of *what, how,* and *for whom to produce.*

Prices in a market economy are determined by supply and demand. Supply refers to the amount of a good or service that businesses will provide at various prices. The law of supply states that more will be supplied at higher than at lower prices. Demand refers to the amount of a good or service that consumers will buy at different prices. The law of demand states that less will be purchased at higher prices than at lower prices. If demand is elastic, a small change in price will cause a large change in quantity demanded. When demand is inelastic, price changes have little effect on quantity demanded.

Supply and demand information can be shown on graphs. Supply curves slope upward. The marginal cost to provide extra units of a good or service increases as more units are produced. The demand curve slopes downward because higher prices reduce people's ability to buy goods and services.

When there is excess demand, the price is bid up by consumers who are unable to get the good or service. When there is excess supply, businesses reduce the price of the good or service. When supply and demand are in balance, there are no forces causing prices to change. The market price is the price at which supply and demand are equal.

In the blank space, write the term that correctly completes the sentence.

elastic
law of demand
excess supply
excess demand
market price
supply
marginal cost
demand curve
law of supply
inelastic

1. A graph that shows the relationship between price and the quantity of a good that consumers want to buy is known as a _____.

2. The _____ is found where the demand and supply curves cross.

3. The _____ states that consumers will buy more of a good or service at lower prices and less at higher prices.

4. _____ is the relationship between price and the quantity of a good that will be offered for sale.

5. The _____ states that firms will produce more of a good at higher prices than at lower prices.

6. The expense of producing an additional unit of output is called _____.

7. Demand is _____ if price changes have little effect on quantity demanded.

8. If producers are offering more for sale at some price than consumers want to buy, _____ is said to exist.

9. If consumers want to buy more of a good than is offered for sale, this condition is called _____.

10. If a price increase causes much less of a product to be demanded, the demand for the product is said to be _____.

REVIEW
QUESTIONS

1. If you have a job that pays you $5 an hour, what would be your opportunity cost, in hours of work, for a new ten-speed bicycle selling for $195?

2. Would you be more concerned about repairing a leaky faucet if your water company charges you for water used by the gallon or a flat rate each month, regardless of the amount used? Why?

3. How do prices send signals to producers and consumers? What do these signals guide?

4. What are two reasons for the law of demand?

5. What is the law of supply, and why does this law hold?

6. If there is excess demand in a market, will the price rise or fall to eliminate that excess demand? Why?

7. Give an example of a product for which demand would be inelastic. Explain.

Profits and Competition

PREVIEW

In the early 1970s, a company named Hewlett-Packard started making hand calculators. These calculators could add, subtract, multiply, divide, and do other mathematical problems, such as compute square roots and take logarithms. Unfortunately, the average student could not afford these products because they cost several hundred dollars each.

Today, many firms are in the business of manufacturing hand calculators, and prices are much lower than they used to be. A device that would have cost several hundred dollars in the early 1970s can now be purchased for less than $30. A simple calculator might sell for as little as $10.

What caused the prices of calculators to drop so much? The answer is competition between the companies that make these products. Each business wants to make additional profits from the sale of calculators. But to increase sales, businesses have been forced to cut their prices.

Profits and *competition* are the key words for this chapter. The heart of the free enterprise system is competition between businesses seeking to increase their profits. In reading this chapter, you will learn why profits and competition are so important in a free enterprise economy. When you have completed the reading and learning activities, you should be able to:

- Describe how profits serve as signals in a market economy.
- Identify the most important uses of profits.
- List four ways by which businesses compete for customers.
- Explain how consumers benefit from competition.

- Define *market power* and explain why it occurs.
- Describe the effects of market power.
- Define the terms *monopoly* and *oligopoly*.

PROFITS

Profits are the dollars left over after a business has paid all of its expenses. Profits serve as payments to persons who invest money and time to start or improve a business.

Entrepreneurs and the Profit Motive

Sometimes a free enterprise system is referred to as a profit system, but it is more accurately called a profit-and-loss system. Several hundred thousand new businesses are started each year. But most of them end up as failures because they are unable to earn enough profit.

Businesses fail for many reasons. In some cases, the reason is that consumers do not want the goods or services being provided. At other times, the product is of poor quality. Some new businesses provide a high-quality product that is in great demand; yet they fail because their costs are so high that they lose money. Still another reason for failure is the lack of business experience of the owners. It is not uncommon for someone with a great idea to fail for lack of an understanding of economics or accounting. Business owners may devote all of their attention to creating the good or service. As a result, they neglect the management of the business.

While most new businesses fail, there are hundreds of success stories. In these cases, good ideas and small amounts of money have created millionaires. Have you ever played an Atari® video game? Hundreds of thousands of these games are in homes all over the world. The Atari company has earned millions of dollars in profits from selling video games and home computers.

Atari was started with a few dollars and an idea. A young man by the name of Nolan Bushnell had an interest in computers. He used his knowledge of electronics to develop video games for pizza palors and game rooms. The games were an instant success. People lined up to zap invading starships and evil monsters. Bushnell realized that there was also a market for video games in homes. He first developed Pong, a product that played tennis-like games when connected to a television set. Later, his Atari company started selling more advanced video games.

Illus. 5-1 *Steven Jobs was one of the entre-preneurs who founded Apple Computing.*

From a garage workshop, Bushnell built a company that sells millions of dollars of games each year. Within the space of just a few years, he went from poor college student to multimillionaire.

People like Nolan Bushnell are called ***entrepreneurs***. The entrepreneurs in a free enterprise system are persons who are willing to take risks to produce profits. Not everyone is cut out to be an entrepreneur. Most people feel more comfortable with a job that provides a guaranteed salary. They know they will never become wealthy, but they are also unlikely to go broke.

Entrepreneurs are different. They are not content with an average standard of living. Instead, most entrepreneurs are willing to risk their money and their talents for a chance to strike it rich. Although entrepreneurs are often in charge of a company, they are different from managers. Usually a manager works for a fixed salary. In contrast, the entrepreneur's payment comes from profits.

A salary is a fixed amount of money. Profits are neither fixed nor guaranteed. It has already been mentioned that most new businesses fail to earn a profit and soon go out of business. If a business fails, the entrepreneur has nothing to show for the investment of money and efforts. If the business turns out to be like Atari, then the rewards to the risk-taker can be very great.

Profits are the prizes that cause entrepreneurs to take risks. People will not take the chance of losing everything unless there is a possibility that they will be big winners. The desire to earn profits is called the *profit motive*. It is the profit motive that drives a free enterprise system.

Suppose there was no chance of earning huge profits. With no rewards, there would be far fewer entrepreneurs. How would a free enterprise economic system be different without risk-takers? For one thing, there would be much less change. Entrepreneurs are the individuals who develop new products and improve old ones. Examples include the Xerox machine, the telegraph, the telephone, the television set, and the assembly-line automobile. Think about how different your world would be without these products. A free enterprise system is kept alive by entrepreneurs and their search for profits.

Profits As Signals

In Chapter 4, you learned that prices act as signals to consumers and producers in a market economy. Profits also provide signals. Specifically, they guide entrepreneurs in deciding how and where to use their talents and money.

Suppose you are an entrepreneur involved in a restaurant that is not making a profit. You are failing to obtain the rewards you expected for your risk-taking. This signals you that your efforts and dollars should be used elsewhere. You become aware that large amounts of profit are being earned by companies selling home computers. The above-average profits being earned by the companies already in that business attract your interest.

Profits are what make a free enterprise system respond to the wishes of consumers. High rates of profit are a signal that consumers like the good or service being provided by a business. They indicate that society desires to have more of its economic resources used to provide that good or service. In a free enterprise economy, entrepreneurs react to this signal and use their dollars and skills to increase the supply of the product.

Low rates of profit or loss indicate that consumers do not approve of the product being provided by a business. They are a signal that resources could be better used in other ways. The signal received by entrepreneurs is that they should shift their attention to another good or service.

Uses of Profits

The profits earned by a business do not all find their way into the entrepreneur's pocket. Although a portion of the profit is often taken by the owner for personal use, a large share of profits is generally put back into the company. Remember that high rates of profit are a signal that society wants more of a company's good or service. Some of the profits earned may be used to buy additional capital goods to produce more of the product. For example, Atari had to use profits to buy more assembly lines. This investment of profits was needed to meet growing consumer demand for video games.

In other businesses, profits may be spent on research intended to improve a product or to develop new ideas. This point is illustrated by the American Telephone and Telegraph Company. AT&T spends millions of dollars each year to support Bell Laboratories. This organization is devoted to research in electronics. The transistor was invented by scientists working at Bell Laboratories. Hundreds of other important ideas have come from these scientists. The profits earned by AT&T on its telephone operations provide the support for this research.

Sometimes profits are used to buy other businesses. A large computer company may buy a small maker of computers with a promising new product. A grocery chain might buy a trucking company to deliver food to each store. In each case, the buying firm sacrifices present profits for future potential profits.

Instant Replay

Profits are the money left over after a business has paid all its expenses.

Entrepreneurs are people who take risks to earn large amounts of money. Their quest for profits is called the profit motive.

High profits signal entrepreneurs that consumers want more of a good or service.

COMPETITION

How would you go about buying a new car? First you might decide what kind of car you want. Suppose a new Ford seems right for you, and there are four Ford dealers within easy driving distance. From which dealer will you purchase your car? It is likely that you will do some price shopping. You will haggle with each dealer to find out who will give you the best price. The successful dealer will probably be the one who offers the lowest price.

The car dealers are aware that you are looking for the best deal. They know that they must beat the prices of the other dealers. Setting a high price is of no value to them if they don't sell any cars. As a result, they cut their prices to persuade you to buy their car. If they fail to get your business, this is a signal that their prices are too high. As a result, the next customer who comes along may be offered a slightly lower price.

The car dealers are in *competition* for car sales. Competition refers to the efforts by businesses to attract customers. The consumer dollars available for buying cars are scarce, and sellers are in a contest to see who can win the largest amount of those dollars. In this contest, consumers are free to use their dollars wherever they get the best deal. Sellers are free to use any legal means to persuade the consumer to buy from them.

Types of Competition

In a football game, the objective is to score points. Points can be scored in several ways. A player can kick a field goal. The quarterback could toss a long pass for a score. The star running back may break loose for an 80-yard run, or the defense could tackle the opposing quarterback in the end zone for a safety.

Competition is a contest between businesses. The objective is to earn more profits. As with football, there are a number of ways that companies can gain customers and earn profits. Some of the most important forms of competition are discussed below.

Price Competition. A company can compete by cutting its prices below those of competitors. Look in your local newspaper. You will see supermarkets advertising a "great buy" on chicken thighs, bread, TV dinners, or even soda pop. You will find discount stores claiming the "lowest prices ever" on cameras, camping gear, thongs, and gardening tools.

Cutting prices requires a trade-off. Lower prices are likely to increase sales. But lower prices also reduce the profit on each sale. The managers of each company must decide on the price that will produce the most profit. Competition will tend to drive prices down until managers believe that it is better to lose some sales than to reduce prices any more.

64

Advertising Competition.   Coca Cola® and Pepsi Cola® are constantly in competition for sales in the soft drink market. Through the years, they have spent millions of dollars on advertising. Advertising is an important form of competition. Companies advertise for two reasons. The first is to convince consumers that they should buy more of the product. For example, Coke and Pepsi ads have the general effect of causing people to drink more soda. The second purpose for advertising is to take sales away from competitors. Coca Cola tries to make you believe that only a Coke will do, while Pepsi Cola claims that people prefer the taste of Pepsi.

Advertising is a substitute for price competition. If a business can convince consumers that it has better products, price cuts may be unnecessary. Consumers may be willing to pay a little more for a well-advertised product. Aspirin is a good example. The ingredients of all brands of aspirin are nearly the same, but advertising makes many consumers willing to pay more for certain name brands.

Quality Competition.   Some businesses compete by trying to offer a superior product. Fine restaurants fit into this category. If you go to one of these restaurants, you know that the bill is going to be high. However, you also know the food is going to be good. It may be worth an extra $5 for a steak if you know that it will not be burned or raw. Good service, a pleasant atmosphere, and a good location may also draw you to the nicer restaurant. The owners of the business are betting their money and efforts that other diners will make a similar choice.

Variety Competition.   Henry Ford was the leading producer of automobiles during the 1920s. In those years, he told consumers they could buy Fords in any color they wanted—as long as they wanted black. Although Fords could be purchased for a very low price, there was no variety. The buyer was stuck with one basic model. Indeed, one of the reasons the price was so low was because only one kind of car was produced. There was no need to use different machines, purchase special paints, or train workers to do a variety of jobs.

Although the early Fords were wonderful cars, not everyone's favorite color was black. Some consumers were willing to pay a higher price to get a car that satisfied them more. As a result, other manufacturers were able to capture a share of the market by offering consumers some choice. Their cars were not necessarily better or cheaper than Fords, but they were different.

Illus. 5-2 *Quality competition is illustrated by fine restaurants competing to provide a superior meal.*

Often, companies can compete successfully by offering consumers a wider range of choice. A clothing store may be successful because it stocks clothing not sold by other stores in the community. For example, in large cities, some clothing stores specialize in outfitting tall, short, or heavy people. There may be stores that offer the latest fashions for teenagers. Others may feature special clothing for religious groups or expensive clothes for the well-to-do. Such stores may not offer an advantage in price or quality. They may not spend much on advertising. They can survive because they meet the special wants of some customers.

Benefits of Competition

Consumers are the winners in the game of competition. The consumer is free to buy a good or service from the seller who offers the best deal. Thus, businesses must try to meet the wants and needs of consumers. Similarly, if the wants and needs of consumers change, competition will force businesses to respond.

Each form of competition benefits consumers. Price competition among sellers results in lower prices as businesses try to win

Economics of Work

customers. Advertising competition, although sometimes confusing, gives consumers information about products and prices. Quality competition forces firms to improve their products. Poor quality goods and services will not be bought, so companies that offer goods or services of poor quality will be forced out of business unless they make improvements. Finally, variety competition gives the consumer a much wider range of choice. Because people have different wants and needs, it is impossible to satisfy everyone with a single type of product. Competition causes companies to seek out and meet the wants of small groups of consumers. These people are better off than if they were forced to select from a narrow range of goods and services.

Competition is important for the efficient use of society's scarce resources. Companies offering products that are not accepted are forced out of business. Businesses that use resources wastefully have high costs, so they must become more efficient or go out of business.

Instant Replay

Competition refers to efforts by businesses to attract customers.

Methods of competing include cutting prices, advertising, improving quality, and offering a greater variety of goods and services.

Competition results in lower prices, more information, higher quality, and greater variety for consumers.

MARKET POWER

If consumers can take their business somewhere else, businesses are forced to compete for sales. However, a company may be the only seller of a good or service, or there may be only a few other sellers. If so, there is little pressure to compete. Businesses that are not faced with the need to compete are said to have **market power**.

For example, suppose you decide to build a house. If there is only one cement company within a hundred miles of where you live, that company has market power. The cost of hauling cement makes it unlikely that you will select a distant cement supplier. The importance of cement in home construction also makes it unlikely that you can find a substitute product. Hence, the local company has power over the market for cement. It doesn't have to cut prices, advertise, worry about quality, or offer a variety of cement types, because the buyers have no real alternative.

Causes of Market Power

Why is there great competition for the sales of some goods and services and little competition for others? There are a number of reasons why some firms gain market power.

Superior Skill.   All businesses are not equally efficient. Some may have the advantage of superior managers. These individuals cause the products to be produced and sold for lower prices than those of competitors. As a result, the other companies are forced out of business. The efficient firm is left as the only seller of the good or service.

Resource Control.   Some goods require special resources for their manufacture. A good example is aluminum. One of the basic ingredients in aluminum is a substance called bauxite. Bauxite is mined from the earth, but it is found in only a few locations. Until World War II, a company called Alcoa owned all of the bauxite mines in the United States. Alcoa had market power over the sale of aluminum. Alcoa's total control was finally ended by the government because of urgent needs for aluminum during the war.

Sometimes the resource controlled by a firm with market power is a good location. A McDonald's next to a high school may have an advantage because students find it easy to walk there for lunch. A Burger King four blocks away may do much less business because its location is less favorable.

Economies of Scale.   Some products can be produced much more efficiently by large firms. A local garage could never make automobiles as cheaply as General Motors. When thousands of cars are produced each day, it is possible to use machines that small car makers could not afford. These make it possible to produce large numbers of items more cheaply than if only a few were made. This is known as *economies of scale*. Because of this, only large companies can survive in the automobile manufacturing business. Large companies are able to produce at lower costs

Illus. 5-3 *Large automobile manufacturers can reduce the cost of producing cars by using industrial robots.*

because of economies of scale. These economies bring down the cost of production. Thus, economies of scale can give a company market power.

Advertising Effects.   A company can develop market power by advertising. If consumers believe one company's product is better than other products, market power can result. The aspirin case mentioned previously is a good example. Advertising has caused consumers to believe that name-brand aspirins are better than so-called "no-name" or generic brands.

Government Assistance.   Often, assistance from the government enables a company to have market power. Electric companies are an example. How many different electric companies sell power in your community? In all but a few locations, there is only one supplier of electricity. One of the reasons is that there are economies of scale in producing electricity. Even more important is the fact that only one company has the legal right to sell electricity. Thus, a company's market power can result partially from a government ruling that eliminates competition. Electric, natural gas, and cable television companies are other examples of businesses protected from competition by government.

Problems Created by Market Power

Competition works to the benefit of consumers. Market power, on the other hand, may not benefit the consumer. When companies have less need to compete for sales, they have less reason to respond to consumers' needs and wants.

Competition keeps prices down. But, when a company has market power, it is under less pressure to keep prices low. The next time you go to a movie, compare the prices of drinks in the theater with those at McDonald's. Once you are inside the movie house, the managers of that business have market power. You are no longer able to go somewhere else to get a drink. The result is that the price of a soft drink is higher than where competition exists.

Competition forces companies to improve the quality of their products. However, a company with market power may worry less about quality. Because the consumer's ability to buy elsewhere is limited, complaints may be ignored. Think about a television repair shop. If there is only one in town, the owner of a broken television set is forced to use that service. The quality of repairs may not be very good, but a lack of choice creates market power. If a new shop opens, the old repair center will have to improve or go out of business.

Competition results in the offering of a great variety of goods and services to consumers. Companies with market power may provide only a narrow range of products. It was competition that finally forced Henry Ford to start making different models and colors of automobiles.

Monopoly and Oligopoly

When there is only one company that supplies a good or service, that firm is called a *monopoly*. The term comes from the Greek language and means "single seller." Monopolists have a great deal of market power. As the only seller, the monopolist does not have to worry about competitors. The firm can set its price at the level that provides the maximum profit. Consumers must either pay the price set by the monopolist or go without the good or service.

For a firm to be a monopoly, two conditions must be met. First, it must be the only convenient seller of a good or service. The cement company mentioned earlier was a monopoly because, although there were other cement companies, they were so far away that they could not effectively compete.

The second condition is that there be no good substitutes for the product sold by the monopoly. If the house in the example

Illus. 5-4 *When only one cafeteria is available in a school or company, consumers' ability to buy elsewhere is limited.*

could be built by using stone or steel, then the local cement company would not be totally free from competition. If the company's price of cement was too high, builders could use the other materials to build the house. Hence, the availability of these substitutes would limit the market power of the cement company.

In some markets there are only a few sellers. A market with few important sellers is called an *oligopoly*. Oligopolies are much more common in the United States than are monopolies. Many important products in the Unitd States are produced in markets with a small number of sellers. The automobile industry is an oligopoly. About 97 percent of all the cars sold in the United States are made by eight firms—General Motors, Chrysler, Ford, American Motors, Toyota, Volkswagen, Nissan, and Honda. Copper mining and the manufacture of rubber are also oligopolies. In each case, over 80 percent of all sales are made by the eight largest firms.

Firms in an oligopoly must compete with one another. However, they often develop their own style of competition. Sometimes they avoid competing on price but spend large sums on advertising. On other occasions they may avoid any form of active competition by agreeing on prices and other matters. When oligopolists stop competing, consumers are the losers.

Instant Replay

Businesses that have little competition are said to have market power.

A business may have market power because of superior skills of its management, control over important resources, economies of scale, advertising, or government assistance.

Firms with market power may charge higher prices, be less concerned with the quality of their products, and offer less variety than firms that are forced to compete.

A single seller of a good or service is called a monopoly. An industry with only a few sellers is referred to as an oligopoly.

SUMMARY

Profits represent the amount remaining after a business has paid its other bills. Most new businesses fail, but some can provide huge profits for their owners. Individuals who risk failure to earn large profits are called entrepreneurs. These persons are important in a free enterprise economy because they assist in the development of new ideas and products. The desire of entrepreneurs to earn profits is referred to as the profit motive.

Profits act as signals in a market economy. High profits signal entrepreneurs that they can benefit by using their time and money to produce a particular good or service. Low profits indicate that their time and money could be better used elsewhere. Profits are used to enlarge the business, to pay for research activities, and to purchase other businesses.

Competition is the effort by businesses to win consumer dollars. Companies compete in a number of ways, including cutting prices, advertising, offering better quality products, and providing consumers with additional choices. Consumers benefit from competition. Society also benefits because scarce economic resources are used more efficiently.

When companies do not have to compete vigorously, they are said to have market power. Market power occurs because some businesses have superior managers or control of scarce resources. Economies of scale, the effects of advertising, and help from the government can also lead to market power. Higher prices, lower quality, and less choice tend to result from market power.

A single seller of a good or service is called a monopoly. An industry with only a few important sellers is referred to as an oligopoly. Firms in an oligopoly often try to avoid competing with one another.

BUILDING YOUR VOCABULARY

profit
entrepreneurs
profit motive
competition
market power
economies of scale
monopoly
oligopoly

In the blank space, write the term that correctly completes the sentence.

1. The risk-takers in an economic system are called _____.

2. An industry with only a few major sellers is an _____.

3. The money left over after a company has paid its expenses is _____.

4. When businesses try to attract buyers to their products, this is called _____.

5. The desire to earn profits is the _____.

6. When products are produced more efficiently by large firms, this is due to _____.

7. Businesses that have little need to compete are said to have _____.

8. When only one company provides a good or service, it is said to be a _____.

REVIEW QUESTIONS

1. How do profits act as signals to entrepreneurs?
2. How are profits used?
3. How can advertising be used as a substitute for price competition?
4. Why does competition among firms usually result in a greater variety of goods and services for consumers?
5. Why do economies of scale provide an advantage for large firms?
6. Aside from the possibility of becoming rich, are there any other reasons that people would want to spend their lives as entrepreneurs?
7. Should the government limit the amount of profits that can be earned by a business? Why or why not?

© 1950, 1952 United Feature Syndicate, Inc.

Business Ownership

"The business of America is business."

— *Calvin Coolidge*

PREVIEW

In the United States, there are about 15 million businesses. This total includes more than 200,000 grocery stores, a similar number of service stations, and about 50,000 drugstores. Some of these businesses are very small. For example, a newsstand on a corner in New York City may be operated entirely by a single owner. The business may consist of a wooden shelter and a magazine rack. Items for sale may be limited to today's newspapers and a few dozen magazines, while the money to run the business may consist of a pocketful of coins for making change.

In contrast, some businesses have become very large. Based on the number of employees, General Motors is the largest firm in the United States. More than 700,000 workers collect their paychecks from this company.

There are many differences between General Motors and the corner newsstand. Size is the most obvious, but another important difference involves the legal rights and responsibilities of the owners. These rights and responsibilities are determined by the form of ownership.

In this chapter, you will learn about owning small and large businesses. When you have completed the reading and the learning activities, you should be able to:

- Explain what is meant by a *sole proprietorship*, a *partnership*, and a *corporation*.
- Explain the advantages and disadvantages of the sole proprietorship, the partnership, and the corporation.
- Describe how *franchises* and *cooperatives* operate.

Illus. 6-1 *A business can be huge like General Motors or it can be a small concession stand on a street corner.*

OWNING A BUSINESS

Have you ever thought about owning your own business? What would you sell? How would you get the money necessary to begin? Whom would you ask to help?

Suppose your favorite aunt leaves you her secret recipe for fudge. You decide you could earn a lot of money by making the fudge and selling it to local candy stores.

What will you need to get started? First, you must have a place equipped for candy-making. Perhaps your parents would be willing to let you use their kitchen. Next, you will need money to buy sugar, chocolate, nuts, and other ingredients to get started. The money you have stashed away for a summer vacation may be enough to get going.

In the beginning, you may be able to take care of everything by yourself. At first, you should have plenty of time to make the fudge and deliver it to the stores. Later, after you get busy, you may have to hire some friends to help you fill orders. Your parents may also decide that they want their kitchen back. As a result, you will have to find another location for your business. You will also need a stove, mixer, refrigerator, and other equipment. Unless you have a pile of money socked away, you may have to borrow from friends, parents, or the bank.

At this point your candy business is called a **sole proprietorship**. This means you are the only owner of the business. Any other people who work for you are your **employees**. An employee is a worker whose wages or salary are set by agreement with the owner. An employee's income is usually not affected by how much profit is earned by the business. **Wages** are amounts paid for periods of work, usually according to the number of hours worked. **Salary** is a regular income paid at set time periods, such as weekly or monthly. Salaries usually do not depend on the number of hours worked.

The owner of a sole proprietorship is entitled to all of the profits of the business. These profits need not be shared with anyone. However, the owner is also responsible for any losses that might result. If your candy business doesn't sell enough fudge to cover expenses, you, as owner, must still pay the bills. If a lot of money is involved, you could be forced to sell your car or some other personal possession.

To be optimistic, suppose the fudge business does very well. You decide to expand and open your own candy stores. One of your first needs will be more money—a lot more money. Another need is for someone to share the risk. A bigger operation can generate more profits, but it can also mean more losses. A third need is for someone to do the bookkeeping. You may be an excellent candy-maker, but might not be good with numbers.

Because of these needs, you decide to take on a partner. After a short search, you find someone who has some money to invest in the candy business. Luckily, this person also has a college degree in accounting. When the two of you have joined together, the business becomes a **partnership**. Although only two partners are in your business, a partnership may involve any number of people. The feature that makes a business a partnership

76

is that several people share ownership. They also share the profits and the responsibilities for any losses of the business.

You soon learn that your new partner has some great ideas. She understands not only accounting but how to sell fudge. As a result, the business really starts to take off. To keep growing, you now need a full-scale candy factory, delivery trucks, and an advertising campaign. Your partner estimates that a million dollars should do the job.

At this point, you and your partner start to get cold feet. The possibility of having to repay a million dollars is just too frightening. Looking for ideas, you go to your lawyer.

The lawyer suggests that the best approach is to form a corporation. A **corporation** is a special form of business that is owned by several people, each of whom has limited liability. **Limited liability** means that each owner cannot lose more than she or he has invested in the business. For example, if you had put $500 into the corporation, that is the most that you could lose. Even if the company lost the entire million dollars, your possible loss is limited to $500. Because of limited liability, it is often easier to find investors for corporations than for partnerships.

The fudge business started out as a sole proprietorship, became a partnership, and finally ended up as a corporation. Not all businesses go through all three forms of ownership. However, many large corporations began as sole proprietorships or partnerships. For example, J.C. Penney Company, Inc., and F. W. Woolworth Co. both started out as sole proprietorships.

Usually, a sole proprietorship or partnership is not the right form of ownership for a very large business. Similarly, most new businesses do not start out as corporations. Each form of ownership has its advantages and disadvantages. In the next sections you will learn more about sole proprietorships, partnerships, and corporations.

Instant Replay

A sole proprietorship is a business owned by one person.

A partnership is a business that has two or more owners. In most partnerships, each person has unlimited liability.

A corporation is a form of business ownership that allows its owners to have limited liability; that is, they cannot lose more than they have put into the business.

SOLE PROPRIETORSHIPS

The sole proprietorship is the simplest form of business organization. The large number of sole proprietorships suggests that there are advantages to this type of business. However, there are some disadvantages as well.

Advantages

- *Easy to start.* Forming a sole proprietorship often requires little more than deciding to go into business. A license may be required but is usually easy to obtain.
- *No sharing of profits.* Any profits that are earned by the business belong to the owner.
- *Own boss.* The owner is totally responsible for decisions about the business. There is no need to get agreement from other people.

Disadvantages

- *Difficult to expand.* Owners of a sole proprietorship often have difficulty in finding money to expand the business. The average person rarely has enough savings to meet the needs of a growing business.

Illus. 6-2 *This florist shop is a sole proprietorship.*

- *Unlimited liability.* Although the owner does not have to share profits, he or she also has no one to help share losses. The owner of a business that fails can lose the money invested in the business. The owner's personal possessions can also be taken if the business itself cannot repay the losses.
- *Limited management skills.* Few people are equally capable in all of the skills necessary to manage a business. The owner of a sole proprietorship may lack some of the important skills of management.

PARTNERSHIPS

Businesses are formed as partnerships for a number of reasons. Friends or relatives become partners because they have trust and confidence in one another. In other businesses, the partnership results from a blending of the partners' skills. Sometimes the partnership is created by the need for money. A poor inventor who joins with a wealthy banker to form a business is an illustration. Partnerships have their own advantages and disadvantages.

Illus. 6-3 *Friends may become partners because they have trust and confidence in one another.*

Advantages

- *Easier to expand.* A rich partner may be able to provide the dollars to allow a business to grow.
- *Sharing of risk.* If the business fails, the losses are the shared responsibility of all the partners.
- *More management skills.* The partners in a business can each use her or his special skills to make the business successful. It is no longer necessary for a single owner to do all management jobs.

Disadvantages

- *Sharing of profits.* Each of the owners receives only part of the profit of the firm.
- *Unlimited liability.* Suppose a partnership involves the poor inventor and the wealthy banker mentioned above. Although both persons are responsible for any losses, the banker has much more to lose. If the inventor can't repay his or her share of the losses, the banker is legally responsible for those losses.
- *Shared decision making.* Partners must agree on decisions about the business. Disagreements are not unusual in a partnership. Sometimes they can become so serious that the individuals are no longer willing to work together.
- *Dissolving the partnership.* If one partner wants to get out of the business, it may be difficult for the firm to continue. One reason is because the partner may have had special skills that are difficult to replace. Also, the remaining partners may not have enough money to buy out the departing partner.

Instant Replay

Sole proprietorships are easy to start and give the owner total control of the business. However, they are difficult to expand, and the owner has unlimited liability.

Partnerships allow sharing of risk and provide for additional management skills. Disadvantages include unlimited liability and problems with dissolving the business.

CORPORATIONS

An early Supreme Court decision stated that corporations have the same rights in their business dealings as individuals. This means that corporations can buy and sell property, enter into contracts, sue, and be sued.

To start a corporation, the owners must first obtain a **charter** from the state in which the business is to be located. The charter lists:
- The name of the corporation
- The purpose of the business
- The amount of money that is being invested to get the business started
- The names of the governing body or **board of directors**

The owners of a corporation are its **stockholders**. A stockholder owns part of a corporation. Ownership is represented by a document called a **stock certificate**. A stock certificate contains the name of the owner and lists the number of shares owned. A **share** in a corporation is a unit of ownership.

Sometimes stockholders are involved in the management of the corporation, but often their role is limited to investing money. Some businesses have many stockholders. For example, American Telephone and Telegraph Company has some three million owners of its stock. Clearly, three million people cannot be involved in day-to-day business decision making.

The use of the corporate form of ownership has made large-scale business possible. The reasons should be clear as you learn about the advantages and disadvantages of the corporation.

Illus. 6-4 *Ownership in a corporation is represented by a stock certificate; stockholders participate in stockholders' meetings.*

Advantages

- *Much easier to expand.* Corporations can rely on a large number of people for money. Some corporations have billions of dollars invested by their owners.
- *Limited liability.* One reason people are willing to invest in a corporation is because their maximum loss is limited. The most any owner can lose is the amount of money invested. No matter how much money the corporation loses, the investor's personal possessions are safe.
- *Ease of transferring ownership.* When an owner of a partnership dies, his or her relatives may want their shares of the business in cash. With a partnership, this may disrupt the business. However, in a corporation it is usually a simple matter to sell stock. Buying and selling of stock is discussed in Chapter 9.
- *Many management skills.* Corporations allow businesses to grow to large sizes. Such large businesses can hire managers with the skills necessary to meet the many different needs of the business.

Disadvantages

- *More taxes.* A government charter gives a corporation special rights. In return, a special tax is applied to the profits of corporations. Typically, the total taxes due on corporate profits are greater than for proprietorships or partnerships.
- *More government regulations.* To protect stockholders and consumers, corporations must comply with government regulations. Many of these regulations do not apply to other forms of business.
- *Little owner control.* The American Telephone and Telegraph Company has three million stockholders. However, no single person or organization owns as much as 1 percent of AT&T stock. As a result, the owners have little to say about the operation of the firm. Like most large corporations, AT&T is controlled by its managers and board of directors.

The Importance of the Corporation

Sole proprietorships, partnerships, and corporations are the three most important forms of business ownership in the United States. Of these three, sole proprietorships are the most common. Figure 6-1 shows that about 70 percent of United States businesses have a single owner. About 10 percent are partnerships, and 20 percent are corporations.

Although there are many more sole proprietorships than corporations, corporations make most of the sales. Figure 6-1 shows

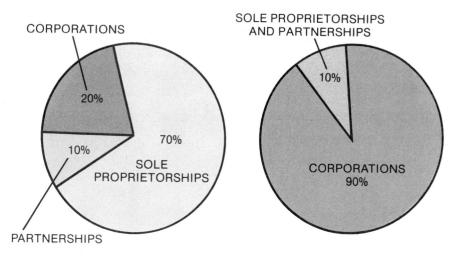

CORPORATIONS

20%

10%

70%
SOLE
PROPRIETORSHIPS

PARTNERSHIPS

**TOTAL NUMBER
OF BUSINESSES**

SOLE PROPRIETORSHIPS
AND PARTNERSHIPS

10%

CORPORATIONS
90%

**TOTAL DOLLAR SALES
BY BUSINESSES**

Figure 6-1 *Only about 20 percent of all United States businesses are corporations; yet they receive about 90 percent of all dollars spent on goods and services.*

that about 90 percent of all dollars spent on goods and services go to corporations. The reason is that corporations are usually much larger than sole proprietorships.

Each year, *Fortune* magazine publishes a list of the 500 largest corporations in the United States. These firms are sometimes called the "Fortune 500." Table 6-1 shows the top ten corporations for 1986. General Motors, the automaker, was the largest. It sold over $100 billion in cars and automotive products in 1986. If you look carefully at Table 6-1, you will notice that six of the ten largest United States firms were involved in producing either oil or autos. The list indicates the importance of the automobile in our modern society.

Table 6-1 *This table shows the order in terms of sales of the top ten Fortune 500 companies in 1986.*

Ten Largest Corporations in the United States (1986)

Rank	Company	Sales (billions of dollars)
1	General Motors	$102.8
2	Exxon	69.9
3	Ford Motor	62.7
4	International Business Machines	51.3
5	Mobil	44.9
6	General Electric	35.2
7	American Telephone & Telegraph	34.1
8	Texaco	31.6
9	E.I. du Pont de Nemours	27.1
10	Chevron	24.4

OTHER FORMS OF BUSINESS OWNERSHIP

Sole proprietorships, partnerships, and corporations are the most
important forms of business ownership in the United States, but
there are two other types of ownership that you should understand.

Franchises

A *franchise* is a business that purchases supplies from and uses
the name of a parent firm. For example, most McDonald's restaurants are franchises. The local McDonald's in your town is
probably owned by someone who lives in your community.
However, McDonald's Corp. has given that person the right to use
the name *McDonald's* and the McDonald's Golden Arches.

Franchises are very common in the United States. This form
of ownership is widely used in the fast-food business and in the
automobile industry. The Burger King Corp. and Wendy's International, Inc., use a franchise agreement in setting up local
restaurants. Similarly, the Chevrolet, Ford, and Toyota dealers in
your community are franchises of the corporations that make
those cars.

Both the parent firm (franchisor) and the local owner (franchisee) can benefit by a franchise agreement. The local franchisee
benefits because she or he can use a well-known, popular name.
People are more likely to go to a Burger King than they are to Joe's
Hamburger Shack. Also, the franchisor usually spends millions of

Illus. 6-5 *This bookstore is an example of a franchise.*

dollars each year on advertising. This advertising helps the local business sell its product.

The parent firm benefits because it receives money from the local business. Usually there is a fee that must be paid in order to use the firm's name. In addition, the franchise often is required to share its profits with and to buy supplies from the parent firm.

Cooperatives

A *cooperative* is a business owned by the people who use its services. Most cooperatives are based on four main principles. First, anyone is allowed to join. A person's sex, race, religion, or nationality makes no difference. Second, people buy ownership shares. These shares give them voting rights in the cooperative. However, each member has only one vote in deciding how the business is to operate. Third, goods and services are sold to all buyers at the same price. The members of the cooperative do not receive a special low price.

Finally, any profits earned by the organization are used to improve the business or are paid back to the members. But the amount of profit received by a member is not determined by how many shares of stock are owned. Rather, the amount is based on how much use the person makes of the cooperative. For example, a person who spends twice as much money on goods and services from the cooperative as another person would receive twice the profits.

Some cooperatives are formed to sell the goods and services produced by their members. These are called *producer cooperatives*. By banding together, the producers of goods and services may be able to persuade buyers to give them higher prices. Ocean Spray® Cranberries, Sun-Maid® Raisins, and Welch's® Grape Juice are examples of producer cooperatives.

Other cooperatives exist for the purpose of buying goods and services. These are called *purchasing cooperatives*. Again, the advantage is size. By buying as a group, members of a cooperative may be able to obtain better prices. Some grocery stores are organized as purchasing cooperatives. Because they buy food in large quantities, they are able to get low prices. Another type of purchasing cooperative involves farmers. These organizations allow the farmers to obtain farm supplies at lower prices.

Instant Replay

A franchise is a business that uses the name of a well-known firm. In return, the franchise makes payments to the parent firm.

Cooperatives are businesses owned by their members. By joining together, the members can sell goods and services that they produce at higher prices or buy goods and services that they need at lower prices.

SUMMARY

Proprietorships are easy to start, do not require the sharing of profits, and allow the owner to make decisions. However, they are difficult to expand. They leave the owner with unlimited liability for losses, and they may have limited management skills.

Advantages of a partnership include sources of money for expansion, the sharing of risk, and more management skills. The disadvantages include sharing profits, unlimited liability of each partner for all losses, problems of shared decision making, and keeping the business going if one partner quits or dies.

Corporations are important in the modern economic system because they can obtain money for expansion from many investors, because they offer those investors limited liability, because ownership in a corporation is easily transferred by the sale of stock, and because the corporation can hire people with specific management skills. On the other hand, corporate profits are taxed more heavily. Corporations have to deal with more government regulations, and corporations may leave their owners with little control over the business.

About 70 percent of all businesses in the United States are sole proprietorships. However, most of these are very small. About 90 percent of all sales are made by corporations.

The owner of a local franchise has the right to use the name of a well-known firm. In return, the franchise must make payments to the parent firm. Cooperatives are owned by the people that use them. Producer cooperatives exist to sell goods and services at higher prices. Purchasing cooperatives can buy goods and services for their members at lower prices.

BUILDING YOUR VOCABULARY

sole proprietorship
limited liability
stockholders
partnership
board of directors
franchise
corporation
cooperative
share
stock certificate
employees
wage
salary

In the blank space, write the term that correctly completes the sentence.

1. A business owned by two or more people, each with unlimited liability, is called a _____.

2. A unit of ownership in a corporation is a _____.

3. _____ are the owners of a corporation.

4. Workers who receive a salary or wage are _____.

5. A _____ is a business owned by one person.

6. A _____ is an amount paid depending on the time worked.

7. A _____ is a business owned by those who use its services.

8. A _____ shows ownership in a corporation.

9. The _____ is the governing body of a corporation.

10. _____ means losses are limited to the amount invested.

11. A _____ is a form of business considered to have many of the same rights as a person.

12. A _____ is a payment for work over a period of time.

13. A local business that uses the name of a well-known firm is a _____.

1. What is meant by unlimited liability?
2. Is it possible that the owners of a corporation may have little to say about the actual operation of the business? Explain.
3. In terms of sales, what is the most important type of business ownership?
4. Four types of information must be provided for a firm to get a charter as a corporation. What are they?
5. List two advantages of a corporation in comparison to a partnership.
6. In what ways is a corporation like a person?
7. How does a franchise agreement benefit the local businessperson?
8. How can producer cooperatives benefit their members? Give an example.

Earning a Living in the Nineties

"If your outgo is greater than your income, then your upkeep will be your downfall."

PREVIEW

The choices you are making now can be very important in determining your future job opportunities. Suppose you want to be a doctor. You must get good grades in high school and college. If you don't work hard for top grades, there is little chance that you will get into medical school. If you prepare yourself for a career in which there are few jobs, you could find that you have wasted your time. If you enter the job market without special skills, you may be unable to get anything but a low-paying job.

This chapter considers job opportunities in the 1990s. It also discusses the ways in which people earn their incomes. When you have completed the reading and the learning activities, you should be able to:

•Explain what determines the demand for different types of jobs.
•Determine which occupations will offer the best career opportunities in the 1990s.
•Find the information you need about careers and career opportunities.
•Explain why some jobs pay higher wages than other jobs.
•Describe the main sources of people's incomes.

THE DEMAND FOR JOBS

From Chapter 4, you know that demand curves for goods and services are downward-sloping. This means that more is demanded at lower than at higher prices. A demand curve can also be developed for labor. Figure 7-1 shows a demand curve for coal miners. It indicates the number of coal miners that mine owners will be willing to hire at different prices. The price of labor is called the wage. For example, Figure 7-1 indicates that, at a wage of $10 per hour, 60,000 miners are demanded.

The Derived Demand for Labor

How do the owners of a business decide the number of workers they want to hire? Think about why a business has employees. The employees help in making the products of the business. The number of workers needed depends on the number of products the business is able to sell. If no one will buy the product, there is no need for employees. But, if the demand for the product is more than the business can supply, the company should expand. This expansion will require more workers.

Consumers buy goods and services to satisfy their needs and wants. Businesses hire workers to produce those goods and services. Thus, the number of workers a business will need is determined by consumer demand for its product. Because of this relationship, labor is said to be a *derived demand*. This means that the demand for workers is derived, or determined, by the demand for the product.

Figure 7-1 *This graph shows a demand curve for coal miners.*

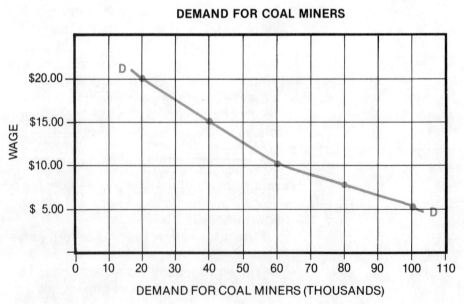

DEMAND FOR COAL MINERS

Economics of Work

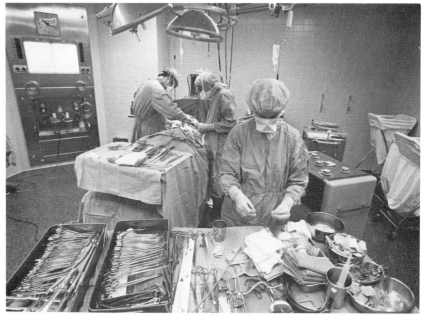

Illus. 7-1 *Quality nurses are in great demand by hospitals.*

The Jewish Hospital of Cincinnati

Consider the coal miner example. If there are plenty of other fuels, such as oil and natural gas, demand for coal may be low. Consumers will probably choose cleaner fuels if prices are about the same. As a result, the demand for coal miners will not be very great. However, if oil supplies from other countries are cut off and if natural gas becomes scarce, the situation changes. More coal will be used for power generation and for heating. The increase in demand for coal will require many more miners than before. Later, if oil and gas supplies increase, coal use will drop and some coal miners will lose their jobs.

The demand for workers in different occupations is derived from the demand for the goods or services they produce. The demand for carpenters is related to the amount of construction in an area. The number of ski instructors that can find jobs is based on how many people want to take up skiing. Opportunities to teach school depend on the number of young people of school age.

Downward-Sloping Labor Demand Curves

Like a demand curve for goods and services, Figure 7-1 shows that more miners will be demanded at a lower than at a higher wage. If the wage drops from $10 to $5 per hour, then another 40,000 miners will be able to find jobs. On the other hand, if the wage goes up to $15 per hour, then only 40,000 miners will work.

Why is the demand curve for labor downward-sloping? One reason is that the demand curve for the goods and services produced by the workers is downward-sloping. To understand this point, consider a business that is thinking about hiring one more person. Employing this extra worker will allow the company to produce more of its product. But the law of demand states that additional product sales require a lower price. Because the added product sells for less, the new worker's output would have less value. Thus, the business will want to hire extra workers only if they can pay them a lower wage. Downward-sloping demand curves for goods and services cause downward-sloping labor demand curves.

A second reason more workers will be hired only at a lower wage is the *law of diminishing returns*. Diminishing means lowering, or decreasing. In most businesses, extra employees do not add as much output as workers already hired. For example, a single miner might produce five tons of coal a day. Adding a second miner would increase the output to nine tons. A third would raise the total to 12. The extra output produced by the second miner is four tons and that of the third is only three tons. Each extra miner provides a diminishing return to the owners of the business.

Because the extra miners produce less coal, they are less valuable to their company. As a result, the owners of the mine will want to hire them only if they will work for a lower wage. Thus, diminishing returns is a second explanation for downward-sloping labor demand curves.

Instant Replay

The demand for labor is derived from the demand for the goods and services that labor will produce.

The labor demand curve is downward-sloping because of the law of diminishing returns and because the demand curve for goods produced by labor is downward-sloping.

JOB OPPORTUNITIES IN THE 1990s

Your understanding of economics can be put to no better use than in helping you to choose a career. Choosing a career is one of the most important decisions you will have to make in the next few years. It may also be one of the most difficult decisions. Researchers have identified over 20,000 different types of jobs in the United States. Many of them require special training and skills. In some areas the demand for workers will increase greatly in the next few years, while in other fields there will be very few openings.

It is not possible in this chapter to consider the future prospects for all types of jobs. However, this discussion does provide some information about fields in which jobs are most likely to be available in the 1990s.

A Glimpse at Job Prospects

It is often useful to group occupations into categories that include jobs of a similar nature. The following categories are used by the Bureau of Labor Statistics of the federal government.

Professional and Technical Workers. This category consists of highly trained workers such as scientists, engineers, doctors, teachers, pilots, and accountants.

Managers and Administrators. Managers and administrators include workers such as bank officers, buyers, credit managers, restaurant managers, and automobile repair managers. Also included are self-employed business operators.

Figgie International, Inc.

Illus. 7-2 *Whether you choose a professional job such as teaching, or a service occupation such as firefighting, choosing a career is an important decision.*

Sales Workers. Salespeople have the responsibility of persuading consumers, governments, and others to buy goods and services they offer. Insurance, real estate, and car salespersons are examples of occupations in this group.

Clerical Workers. Clerical workers include bank tellers, bookkeepers, secretaries, and cashiers. This group is the largest of the occupational categories.

Craft Workers. Craft workers consist of a wide variety of highly skilled people. Included are carpenters, electricians, machinists, instrument makers, and automobile mechanics.

Operatives. As the name suggests, operatives are workers who operate some sort of equipment. Transportation operatives include bus, truck, and taxi drivers. Other operatives are responsible for heavy equipment such as forklifts and road graders.

Nonfarm Laborers. Construction workers, freight handlers, and garbage collectors are examples of the occupations grouped in this category.

Private Household Workers. Maids, butlers, housekeepers, childcare workers, and gardeners are some of the jobs in this group.

Other Service Workers. This group includes people such as fire fighters, janitors, waiters, and barbers. As the name suggests, workers in this category provide a service rather than help in producing a product.

Farm Workers. Both those who own farms and also those who are hired to work on a farm are classified as farm workers.

The Bureau of Labor Statistics keeps tabs on job opportunities in each of the occupational categories. Figure 7-2 shows the number of new jobs expected between 1984 and 1995. The figure indicates that over 5 million additional jobs for professional and technical workers will be available. However, there will be 182,000 fewer jobs for private household workers and 107,000 fewer jobs for farm workers.

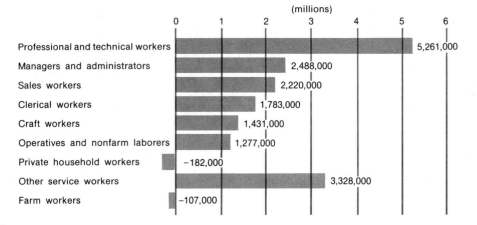

NUMBER OF NEW JOBS: 1984–1995

(millions)

Professional and technical workers	5,261,000
Managers and administrators	2,488,000
Sales workers	2,220,000
Clerical workers	1,783,000
Craft workers	1,431,000
Operatives and nonfarm laborers	1,277,000
Private household workers	–182,000
Other service workers	3,328,000
Farm workers	–107,000

Figure 7-2 *This chart shows the number of new jobs for occupational categories. Which category will have the greatest number of new jobs between 1984 and 1995? Which will have the least?*

Sources of Additional Information

The federal government provides some excellent sources of information on job opportunities and training requirements. The best is the *Occupational Outlook Handbook* of the Bureau of Labor Statistics. This book is published every two years and is probably in your community or school library. It contains information on hundreds of different occupations.

Instant Replay

In some occupations there will be many new jobs in the future. Other occupations will experience employment declines.

The *Occupational Outlook Handbook* is a good source of information about job opportunities and requirements.

SOURCES OF INCOME

A person's income is the total amount of dollars that she or he earned during the year. This income usually comes from one or more of four sources—wages and salaries, rents, interest, and profits. This section discusses each of the four income sources.

Illus. 7-3 *Sources of income include wages earned on a job and rental charges for the use of property.*

Wages and Salaries

Wages and salaries are payment for a person's labor. Clearly, not everyone receives the same amount of money for each hour worked. Differences in wages and salaries for various jobs are mostly determined by the forces of supply and demand. Figure 7-3 shows the supply and demand curves for coal miners. The reason that the demand curve slopes downward has already been explained. The supply curve (marked with an "S" at each end) slopes upward. This means that more people will become coal miners if they can get paid more. This makes sense because, as wages of coal miners increase, more people will want these jobs.

Figure 7-3 *Shown on this graph are the supply and demand curves for coal miners.*

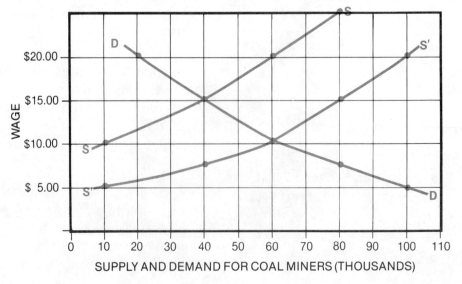

SUPPLY AND DEMAND FOR COAL MINERS

Economics of Work

The *market wage* is determined by where the supply and demand curves cross. If the wage is above the market wage, there will be more applicants than jobs. To get a job, some people will have to go into the mines for less money. If the wage is below the market wage, there is an excess demand for miners. To get enough miners to meet their needs, the mine owners will have to pay higher wages. Only at the market wage does the number of people willing to work as miners equal the demand for miners.

Now suppose that all the high school teachers in the country decided to become coal miners. The result would be that, at each wage, more people would be available to work as miners than before. In Figure 7-3, this shows as a new supply curve—labeled with an "S'" at each end. Note that the curve shows more people willing to work at each wage. For example, the original supply curve indicates 40,000 people willing to be miners at a wage of $15 per hour. The new curve shows that there are 80,000 willing miners at $15 per hour.

As more people want to become miners, the market wage drops. Note that the demand curve and the new supply curve cross at a wage of $10 per hour. This is because, at the old market wage of $15, more jobs are wanted than are offered. Only by accepting lower pay can everyone find a job.

Supply and demand explain why wages are higher in some occupations than in others. As more people want to get jobs in a particular field, the market wage drops. On the other hand, if businesses suddenly require more of a particular type of worker, they must offer higher wages.

Computer programmers and farmhands are good examples of how supply and demand affect wages in different occupations. Computers have become more and more important in society. Hence, the demand for people who can write computer programs has also increased. Because the demand is growing faster than the supply, the market wage for computer programmers has increased.

On the other hand, the demand for farm laborers is actually declining as machines are becoming increasingly important in agriculture. Because the supply of farm workers is declining less rapidly than the demand, the market wage remains low.

Supply and demand also explain the high salaries that are paid to star professional athletes. Baseball pitchers who fill stadiums each time they pitch are worth a lot of money to team owners. Unfortunately, there are only a few of these pitchers available. Because the demand is great and the supply very limited, such players receive high salaries.

Rents

People who own resources such as land are able to charge *rent* for use of the resources. Like wages, rents are determined by supply and demand. A piece of desert property may have a low rental value because much is available and little is demanded. On the other hand, a small piece of land in New York may rent for 100,000 times as much as the desert land. The very limited amount of space available causes the price to be bid to a high level.

Interest

The *interest rate* is the price that lenders charge for letting others use their money. An interest rate is the amount of money that must be paid, divided by the number of dollars borrowed. For example, if a borrower must pay $10 to borrow $100 for one year, the interest rate is 10 percent. Like all prices, the interest rate is determined by demand and supply. The demand is the amount of money that people want to borrow. Supply is the amount of money available to lend.

Profits

As discussed in Chapter 5, profits are the dollars remaining after all expenses of a business have been paid. Profits represent a payment to the entrepreneurs who risked their talents and money in a business.

Distribution of Income

Table 7-1 shows the proportions of all the income in the United States that comes from each of the four sources. Notice that about 76 cents out of every dollar comes from wages and salaries. In contrast, only 2 percent comes from rents. Remember, however, that these percentages are averages. One person's income may come almost entirely from rents. Another's may come primarily from interest or profits.

Table 7-1 *Shown here are proportions of all income in the United States from each of the four sources.*

Sources of Income in the United States

Source	Percent of Total
Wages and Salaries	76.2%
Rents	2.0
Interest	10.6
Profits	11.2

Economics of Work

Some people have much higher incomes than others. The owner of a large business may make several million dollars a year, while a retired person's income may be under $10,000. Table 7-2 shows the *distribution of income* in the United States. The poorest fifth of the population earns only about 5 percent of the income. At the other extreme, the richest fifth of the population receives about 40 percent, or two-fifths of all income.

Table 7-2 *Shown here is the distribution of income in the United States.*

Distribution of Income in the United States

Category	Percent of Total
Poorest Fifth	4.7%
Second Poorest Fifth	11.1
Middle Fifth	17.1
Second Richest Fifth	24.4
Richest Fifth	42.7

Instant Replay

The labor supply curve, like the supply curve for goods and services, is upward-sloping.

The market wage rate and the amount of labor hired is determined by supply and demand.

The four main sources of income are wages and salaries, rents, interest, and profits.

SUMMARY

The demand for labor is a derived demand; that is, the number of workers businesses will hire is derived, or determined, by the demand for their products. The demand curve for labor is downward-sloping. This is because the demand for goods and services is downward-sloping and also because of diminishing marginal returns.

Occupations can be grouped into broad categories that include jobs of a similar nature. In some occupations employment will grow in the future, while in others fewer jobs will be available. Additional information on several hundred occupations can be found in the *Occupational Outlook Handbook*.

People receive their incomes from wages and salaries, rents, interest, and profits. The wage is the price of labor. The rental rate is the payment for land. The interest rate is the payment for borrowing dollars. Profits are the reward for risking time and money as an entrepreneur. The market prices paid for these economic resources are determined by supply and demand. About three-fourths of all income comes from wages and salaries. There is considerable inequality in people's incomes.

BUILDING YOUR VOCABULARY

Occupational Outlook Handbook
derived demand
distribution of income
market wage
rent
law of diminishing returns
interest rate

In the blank space, write the term that correctly completes the sentence.

1. _____ is a payment for temporary use of land or a building.

2. The _____ shows how many families are in each income category.

3. The _____ is found where the labor demand and supply curves cross.

4. The demand for labor is said to be a _____ because it depends on the demand for the goods and services that the labor will produce.

5. The _____ suggests that as more workers are hired, the additional production of each one will be less than the one hired previously.

6. The _____ is the price of money.

7. A good source of information about jobs is the _____.

REVIEW QUESTIONS

1. Based on the information in Figure 7-1, how many more coal miners would be demanded at $10 per hour than at $15 per hour?
2. In which occupational category would your teacher fit? What about a welder?
3. What are the four sources of income? Which is the most important?
4. If people suddenly decided they wanted to borrow more money, how would this decision affect the interest rate? Explain.
5. Why does the law of diminishing returns cause labor demand curves to be downward-sloping?
6. Which job category will have the most new openings by 1995? The least?

7. How do supply and demand explain the high incomes earned by rock stars?
8. What percent of total income is received by the richest 40 percent of the population?

Labor Unions

"When the union's inspiration through the worker's blood shall run,

There can be no power greater anywhere beneath the sun.

Yet what force on earth is weaker than the feeble strength of one?

But the union makes us strong."

— *Union song:* Solidarity Forever

PREVIEW

Labor unions are an important part of the economic and political system in the United States. About 18 million Americans are union members. This total represents almost one-fifth of all nonfarm employees. In some of the largest industries, almost all workers are union members. Examples include automobile manufacturing, steel making, and coal mining.

Union supporters argue that unions are necessary to make sure that workers are fairly treated by the owners of businesses. Opponents often suggest that unions are a cause of inflation. It is also said that unions resist change to more efficient methods of production and cause economic loss through strikes. In this chapter you will learn about labor unions in the United States.

When you have completed the reading and the learning activities in this chapter, you should be able to:
• Describe the development of labor unions in the United States.
• Explain some of the important laws that affect unions.
• Describe the organization of labor unions.
• List the primary goals of unions.
• Explain the steps involved in forming a union and in collective bargaining.

LABOR UNION HISTORY

A *labor union* is a group of workers who have joined together to improve their economic conditions. The history of unions in the United States goes back nearly 200 years. In 1972, shoemakers in Philadelphia organized a union. Their aim was to reduce their working hours and to set the selling prices of the shoes they made. However, the real beginnings of unionism in the United States can be traced to the Industrial Revolution.

The *Industrial Revolution* occurred in the early 1800s. The term refers to a period when machines were first introduced to replace hand labor. With the Industrial Revolution came large factories. Workers in these factories were often required to work long hours, in unhealthy conditions, and for low wages. An individual worker who complained could easily be replaced by an unemployed person anxious for a job.

To improve their lives, many of the workers banded together to form unions. The oldest existing union in the United States is the International Typographical Union, organized in 1850. Other unions soon followed, involving occupations such as machinists, blacksmiths, stonecutters, and locomotive engineers. Most of these unions started in a particular location, but many grew to include workers from all over the country.

Illus. 8-1 *Early unions worked to improve working conditions in factories.*

National Archives Trust

These individual unions greatly increased the bargaining power of their members. However, some union leaders wanted a single labor organization that could speak for all workers. One early attempt was the Knights of Labor, formed in 1869. Everyone except lawyers, bankers, gamblers, liquor dealers, and detectives were invited to join. The Knights of Labor grew to almost 800,000 members in a few short years. But this organization quickly dwindled and disappeared after it became involved in violent strikes in which several people were killed.

The American Federation of Labor (AFL) was the next important labor organization. Organized by Samuel Gompers, the AFL had three important characteristics. First, it was based on the principle of federalism. This meant that the individual member unions continued to have rights even though they became part of the larger organization. The second characteristic was that the AFL concentrated primarily on improving economic conditions of its members. In contrast, the Knights of Labor had been very involved in politics. Finally, the AFL was an organization of craft unions. A *craft union* involves workers who have particular skills. For example, one craft union might be made up of carpenters. Another would consist only of bricklayers.

For 50 years the AFL was the leading labor organization in the United States. Then, during the Depression years of the 1930s, some AFL leaders wanted to broaden the membership by including industrial union members. An *industrial union* includes all of the workers in an industry. For example, all mine employees, regardless of their jobs, can belong to the United Mine Workers.

A bitter disagreement resulted and, in 1938, a second national labor organization was formed. This was called the Congress of Industrial Organizations or CIO. From 1938 to 1955, the AFL and the CIO existed as rival labor organizations. This rivalry created many problems. Sometimes strikes resulted, not because workers were dissatisfied with their employers, but because of conflicts between the AFL and CIO. In 1955, peace was achieved and the two organizations joined together to form the *AFL-CIO*. Today, the majority of all union members are part of this organization.

Instant Replay

Craft unions involve workers with particular skills, while industrial unions organize workers by industry.

Most union members in the United States belong to the AFL-CIO.

LAWS AFFECTING LABOR UNIONS

As you might expect, the growth of unions was often opposed by the owners of businesses. Many companies simply refused to talk with union leaders. When these leaders directed their union members to strike, managers accused them of breaking the law. In some cases, the courts decided that the activities of the labor leaders were illegal. A number of union officials were put in jail, while others lost their jobs because of their activities. Unions had to fight both their employers and the courts. As a result, unions had a difficult time in the first 50 years after the AFL was formed.

National Labor Relations Act

During the Great Depression of the 1930s, many people were unable to find jobs. As a result, Congress became more aware of the problems of workers and passed laws to help unions. One of the most important was the *National Labor Relations Act* of 1935. This law gave unions a legal right to exist. It guaranteed employees the right to form a union. It also required employers to bargain with union representatives.

In addition, the National Labor Relations Board, or NLRB, was set up to enforce the 1935 law. Union members can appeal to the NLRB if they believe they are being unfairly treated. Appeals can also be made if the owners refuse to bargain with the union. The NLRB can force both employers and unions to obey the law. Today, this agency continues to act as a watchdog over labor-business relations.

Taft-Hartley Act

In the years just after World War II, there were a number of strikes in important industries. The problems created by these strikes left many people feeling that unions had become too powerful. The *Taft-Hartley Act* was passed in 1948 to limit the power of unions. One important part allows the President of the United States to delay a strike. This can be done if the President feels the strike would cause serious problems for the nation. For example, a national railroad strike could cut off supplies of fuel and food for the entire nation. The Taft-Hartley Act gives the President the right to order the workers back on the job for 80 days. This "cooling-off" period provides time for the union and the employers to try to settle their differences.

Another provision of the Taft-Hartley Act made the closed shop illegal. A *closed shop* is one that can hire only members of the union that represents the workers already employed. The closed shop was viewed as unfair because it reduced job opportunities for workers who were not union members.

Related to the closed shop is the union shop. In a *union shop*, nonunion workers can be hired. But these employees must join the union within a short time after they are hired. Opponents argue that the union shop limits the right of individuals to decide whether they want to join a union. Unions respond that all workers gain benefits from union bargaining. Therefore, all workers should have to contribute to the union. Otherwise, nonunion employees would receive benefits for which they didn't pay.

The Taft–Hartley Act did not outlaw the union shop. But it did give individual states the right to pass laws that do so. A state law that outlaws the union shop is called a *right-to-work law*. At present, 21 states have right-to-work laws. They are identified in Figure 8-1. Notice that most of these states are in the South and West. The states in the Midwest and in the East have many union members. These members have succeeded in preventing such laws from being passed. Often, the debate over right-to-work laws is very heated.

Instant Replay

The National Labor Relations Act gave unions the right to organize, while the Taft–Hartley Act limited the power of unions.

Twenty-one states have right-to-work laws that outlaw union shops. Closed shops were prohibited by the Taft–Hartley Act.

UNION ORGANIZATION IN THE UNITED STATES

Most unions are part of the AFL–CIO. However, some labor groups, such as the United Mine Workers and the Teamsters Union, are not AFL–CIO members. They are referred to as independent unions.

Figure 8-2 is an organization chart for the AFL–CIO. It shows that the AFL–CIO is made up of the member national unions. In turn, the national unions are made up of the local unions. The role of each of the three is discussed in this section.

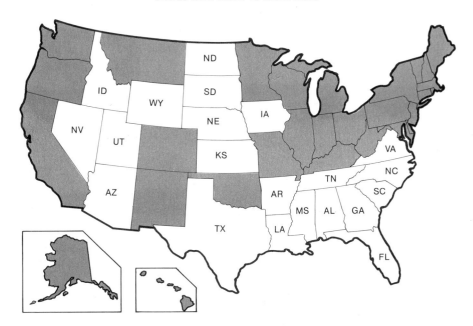

STATES WITH RIGHT-TO-WORK LAWS

Figure 8-1 *States having right-to-work laws are shown in white on this map.*

Figure 8-2 *The AFL-CIO is made up of national unions that are, in turn, made up of local unions.*

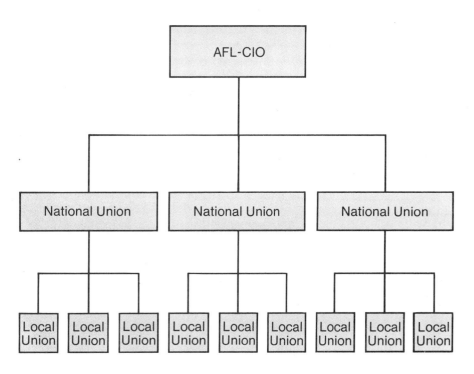

The AFL-CIO

The AFL-CIO is still based on the principle of federalism. It acts as a national voice for labor. But its direct control over union members is limited. Much of the effort of the AFL-CIO attempts to improve the image of unions. The AFL-CIO also works to influence government policies to benefit union members.

National Unions

There are about 200 national unions in the United States. Some are craft unions, and some are industrial unions. Nine national unions have more than a half-million members.

One of the main responsibilities of a national union is to negotiate contracts for its members. A contract is a written agreement that lists the terms of work. Wages, working hours, and job responsibilities are examples of the items covered in a contract.

Local Unions

A worker's real involvement with a union is at the local level. The individual's union membership is in the local union, and it is to the local that dues are paid. Local union members must vote on contracts negotiated by the national union. The leaders of the local union must actually sign these contracts.

There are some 80,000 local unions in the United States. Some have as few as a dozen members. At the other extreme, employees of the Ford Motor Company in Detroit belong to a United Auto Workers local with 30,000 members. However, most local unions have between 50 and 1,000 members.

GOALS OF UNIONS

The general objective of a union is to improve the economic condition of its members. This broad goal can be broken down into five issues of particular interest. Unions attempt to negotiate contracts with the most favorable terms possible in each of the following areas:
- Wages
- Working hours
- Job security
- Fringe benefits
- Working conditions

Wages

Usually, an important objective of unions is to win an increase in wages. During times of increasing prices, union leaders may also try to get a cost-of-living adjustment in the contract. This increases wages as prices rise. It is designed to help workers protect their gains against price increases. In recent years, most union contracts have included a cost-of-living adjustment.

Fringe Benefits

Fringe benefits include days of paid vacation, medical and dental insurance, life insurance, and pensions. Over the past 20 years, such benefits have become more and more important to union members. In 1960, employers paid 21 cents in fringe benefits for every dollar of wages paid. By 1987, the cost had nearly doubled to 37 cents for each dollar of wages.

Working Hours

One of the major achievements of unions has been the establishment of the eight-hour workday. Working hours are still of great interest to most unions. Where wages are high, contract negotia-

Illus. 8-2 *Unions negotiate for better fringe benefits, such as longer paid vacations.*

Virginia State Travel Service

tions may try to reduce the number of working hours. In other cases, questions relating to working hours may be considered. These include when the working day should start and end, the time allowed for lunch, and the number and length of breaks.

Working Conditions

Unions are very concerned about the health and safety of their members. A contract may require that the workplace be clean, well-lighted, and neither too warm nor too cold. It may prohibit the employer from using dangerous chemicals or unsafe machines. The contract may also spell out in great detail the specific responsibilities of different jobs. For example, the duties of welders and machinists may be carefully defined to prevent conflicts on the job.

Job Security

The success of a union is closely related to the number of jobs available for its members. As a result, a union is very aware of changes that could reduce the demand for the skills of its members.

The issue of job security also involves the hiring, firing, and disciplining of individual workers. With respect to hiring, unions want their members to be given the first chance at new jobs. As a result, they push for contracts that give preference to union members. The closed shop and the union shop are examples of efforts to preserve jobs for union members.

With respect to firing and disciplining, the objective of the union is to protect its members. *Grievance procedures* are a way of helping workers who feel they have been treated unfairly. Sometimes the grievance procedure will involve a hearing before a panel consisting of union and management members. In extreme cases, a worker may ask for help from the NLRB.

UNIONS IN ACTION

Suppose you are employed by a business whose workers are not represented by a union. Thinking about your low pay and long hours, you decide that a union could help you and your fellow workers. What would you do next?

There is a way to bring a union into a firm. The workers in a business tell the National Labor Relations Board that they are considering a union. Officials of the NLRB then supervise an election. Every worker is allowed to vote for or against the proposed union. If a majority of the workers vote for the union, the union then has the right to represent employees in contract discussions with the employer.

Once the union has been approved, the next step is to set a time for negotiating a contract. On that day, representatives of the union and of management sit down together and present their proposals. Typically, the union believes that the offer of management is not enough, and the management team usually claims that the union is demanding too much. Hence, the two teams must bargain until they can reach an agreement acceptable to both groups.

If there is no real hope of agreement, the union leaders may decide to call a *strike*. A strike occurs when a group of workers decides to stop working until it gets approval of its demands. Often, striking workers will set up picket lines around their place of employment. *Picket lines* are intended to call attention to the strike. Strikers hope to discourage other workers, businesses, or consumers from dealing with the company.

A strike hurts both the employees and the employer. The workers lose their wages. Although workers may get some financial help from their union, these funds are limited. On the other hand, the owners of the business are also hurt because they can

Illus. 8-3 *Disagreements between unions and employers may lead to a strike.*

"Gimme 14 hot hogs."

no longer produce their product. The employer doesn't have to pay the workers. Because payments still have to be made for expenses such as rent or interest on borrowed money, an employer can have a large loss during a strike.

To a degree, a strike is like playing "chicken." The union hopes the company will become desperate and give in to its demands. The employer may be waiting until the union members have used their savings and must come back to work. Eventually, a compromise is reached and a new contract is signed. Often, however, one side has to give up more than the other. This is the side that has the most to lose if the strike continues.

Discussions between union and management negotiators can be very long, complicated, and sometimes rather heated. However, they usually result in an agreement without the union going on strike. In fact, of the 100,000 contracts that are negotiated each year, only about 5 percent involve a strike. More workdays are lost each year by employees who stay home with colds than from strikes.

However, using nationwide averages can be very misleading. Averages show that during a typical year only about three minutes of each workday are lost to strikes. But the impact on individual businesses and workers can be very serious. Some businesses never recover from a long strike, and some strikers may spend years trying to regain the income lost during a strike. In most cases, a strike is something that neither the company nor the union wants.

Instant Replay

Union elections are supervised by the National Labor Relations Board.

Picket lines are used to call attention to union demands.

Strikes hurt both unions and employers. Most disagreements are resolved without resorting to strikes.

SUMMARY

About 18 million Americans belong to unions. Craft unions involve workers with a particular skill. Industrial unions organize all of the workers in an industry. Most union members in the United States are members of the AFL–CIO. The AFL–CIO is made up of national unions. In turn, these national unions are made up of local unions.

The National Labor Relations Act gave unions a legal right to exist. It also set up the National Labor Relations Board. The NLRB's job is to make sure that unions and management deal fairly with one another.

The Taft-Hartley Act limits the power of unions. It allows the President to delay strikes that would cause serious national problems. It also outlaws the closed shop and allows states to pass right-to-work laws that outlaw the union shop. A closed shop requires that a worker be a union member to get a job. The union shop requires workers to join the union after getting the job.

Wages, fringe benefits, working hours, working conditions, and job security are of special interest to unions in contract negotiations. If unions and management are unable to agree on a contract, a strike may result. Striking workers may also picket the place where they normally work. Most contract disagreements are settled without a strike. But a long strike can cause serious problems for both employers and union members.

BUILDING YOUR VOCABULARY

strike
Industrial
   Revolution
labor union
craft union
closed shop
National Labor
   Relations Act
AFL–CIO
Taft–Hartley Act
union shop
National Labor
   Relations Board
right-to-work laws
grievance
   procedures
picket line
industrial union

In the blank space, write the term that correctly completes the sentence.

1. A law that prohibits closed shops is called the _____.

2. The _____ is an organization made up of national unions.

3. Machines came into wide use in manufacturing during the _____.

4. A group of workers that has organized to improve its wages and working conditions is called a _____.

5. A union consisting of workers with a particular skill is called a _____.

6. A workplace where only union members can get jobs is called a _____.

7. _____ indicate how disagreements between labor and management will be resolved.

8. When workers agree to stop working, a _____ occurs.

9. A _____ is the name given to a group of workers marching in front of a business to call attention to their demands.

10. A workplace where new employees must agree to join a union soon after beginning work is called a _____ .

11. A union that includes all of the workers in a given industry is called an _____.

12. The _____ is a law that gave unions the right to represent workers.

13. State _____ prohibit union shops.

14. The _____ is a government agency designed to assure that management and unions deal fairly with one another.

REVIEW QUESTIONS

1. What was the Industrial Revolution, and how did it affect the development of unions?
2. Is the United Auto Workers a craft union or an industrial union? Explain.
3. Which law gave unions the right to exist and to bargain with employers?
4. How can a closed shop reduce job opportunities for nonunion workers?
5. What are five common union objectives?
6. Why do unions sometimes picket a business?
7. Should public employees such as members of police and fire departments be allowed to strike? Why or why not?
8. If a business is losing money, should union members be willing to work for lower wages? Why or why not?
9. Should people buy goods and services from a business that is being picketed? Explain.

Producing Goods and Services

PREVIEW

Business managers have many day-to-day responsibilities. They must make sure that the materials necessary to produce their product are available. They must be certain that customer orders for the product are being filled. They must hire new workers to replace those who have retired or found other jobs.

Managers are also faced with difficult decisions that can affect the futures of their companies. The president of General Motors may have to decide whether to produce a new model of sports car. This decision could require investment of many millions of dollars in new equipment. The owner of a small computer company may need to find $1,000,000 to keep the business operating.

These situations deal with important business activities. The sports car issue involves the decision to buy capital goods. The computer company manager's problem is meeting the firm's money needs.

This chapter considers business decisions regarding producing goods and services. When you have completed the reading and the learning activities, you should be able to:
- List three factors that determine interest rates.
- Show how interest rates affect the demand for capital goods.
- Describe the differences between stocks and bonds.
- Explain how specialization of labor reduces the cost of producing goods and services.
- Discuss the benefits of automation and mass production.

INVESTING IN CAPITAL GOODS

Chapter 2 explains how human, natural, and capital resources are used to produce goods and services. Many businesses must purchase each type of resource to produce their own products or services. However, the decision to purchase capital resources or goods requires special attention. Such decisions are often affected by interest rates on money borrowed to make the purchases.

Interest Rates

The interest rate is the price of borrowing money. If a company borrows $1,000 and must pay $150 in interest each year, the interest rate is 15 percent (150 divided by 1,000 equals 0.15). If only $100 in interest is due each year, the interest rate is 10 percent (100 divided by 1,000 equals 0.10).

Three basic factors determine interest rates. The first is supply and demand. Remember, the interest rate is the price charged to borrow money. Supply and demand work to determine this price, just as they do any other price.

If the demand for loans is greater than the supply of money available for borrowing, there is excess demand. This will cause interest rates to increase. If, however, the supply of money to loan is greater than the demand, there is an excess supply. This will force interest rates lower. The market rate of interest is the rate at which the supply of and demand for money are equal.

Illus. 9-1 *A bank pays interest on money that is loaned to it.*

Economics of Work

The second factor that affects interest rates is the risk faced by the lender. Risk refers to the chance that the business will be unable to repay the loan. The greater a company's profits, the lower its borrowing risk will be. Hence, lenders evaluate the prospect that a company's profits will grow or at least continue at the same level.

Usually lenders want a higher interest rate if there is more risk involved. For example, American Telephone and Telegraph Company can borrow money at a lower interest rate than you could. The reason is that the banker would assume that AT&T offers a lower risk of loss.

Inflation is the third factor that affects interest rates. Inflation means increasing prices of resources and goods and services. If prices are going up, the dollars repaid are worth less than the money loaned. For example, suppose you borrow $100 today and repay it 10 years later when everything costs twice as much. If costs double, the same money will buy half as much in 10 years as it could today.

Lenders of money are aware that inflation will make their dollars worth less. As a result, they charge higher interest rates if they believe prices are going to increase in the future.

Interest Rates and Investment in Capital Goods

The demand for investment in capital goods is affected by the level of interest rates. The reason is that companies usually borrow money to buy capital goods. When interest rates decrease, the demand for capital goods increases.

Suppose, for example, the managers of a business are considering investing in each of the capital goods listed below. Also suppose each item will cost $100,000. Following each of the capital goods is an amount of money. These are the extra amounts the managers expect the business to earn as a result of buying the capital goods.

- A heating system that will reduce the amount of heating oil used. Benefit: $150,000
- A machine that makes pizza crusts at the rate of 500 per hour. Benefit: $125,000
- A printing press used to print books about economics. Benefit: $110,000

Suppose the company must borrow money to buy these capital goods. How should the managers decide the number of projects in which to invest? The answer depends on the interest rate.

Illus. 9-2 *The demand for investment in capital goods, such as this printing press, is affected by interest rates.*

Assume the company has to pay a very high interest rate, say 40 percent per year, to borrow money. How much money should the firm borrow to buy capital goods? Note that the first project will earn $150,000 and requires that the company borrow $100,000. If the interest rate is 40 percent, the total amount of interest is 40 percent of $100,000, or $40,000. The first project will earn $150,000. Thus, the business can return $100,000 to the lenders, pay the $40,000 in interest, and still have $10,000 left. Clearly, the firm should choose to invest in the first project.

But what about the other investments? Neither of them is a good choice. Suppose the business buys the pizza crust maker. It will have to repay $140,000 (the $100,000 borrowed plus the $40,000 in interest). But it will receive only $125,000 from its investment. The printing press is an even worse investment. The $140,000 spent will return only $110,000. Thus, when the interest rate is 40 percent, only the first project is a good investment. At an interest rate of 40 percent, the demand for capital goods investment will be $100,000 for the first project only.

Now suppose the interest rate drops to 20 percent. The amount of interest on each project drops to $20,000 (20 percent of $100,000) and the total cost is $120,000. At this lower interest rate, the pizza oven is a good choice. Because the investment will bring in $125,000, the company can earn $5,000 after paying its costs.

However, the printing press is still a losing proposition. The business would lose $10,000 if it invested in this particular capital good. So, at an interest rate of 20 percent, the demand for capital goods will be for the first two projects. That is, the total demand will be $200,000.

If the interest rate drops below 10 percent, the printing press should be purchased. This is because repaying the money plus paying the interest will cost less than the $110,000 the press will earn. Thus, at interest rates below 10 percent, all three projects should be selected. The demand for capital goods will increase to $300,000.

Figure 9-1 shows how the demand for investment in capital goods is related to the interest rate. The illustration indicates that investment demand increases as interest rates go down. The reason is that, at lower interest rates, more and more projects involving capital goods become profitable.

Importance of Capital Goods

This relationship between interest rates and the demand for capital goods is very important in the economic system. When interest rates are high, companies do not invest in as many capital goods as when interest rates are lower. But capital goods are used to produce many of the goods and services that satisfy human wants. If interest rates remain high for a long time, a

Figure 9-1 *This graph shows how demand for investment in capital goods relates to interest rates.*

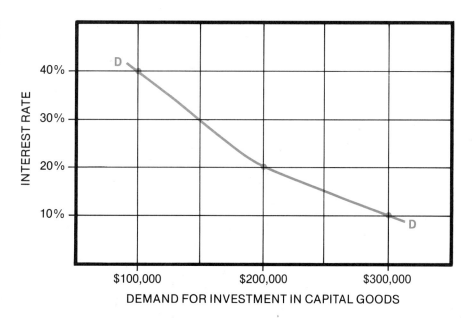

shortage of capital goods results. This shortage may reduce the amount of goods and services that will be available for consumers in the future.

Electricity is an example of this problem. If interest rates are high, electric companies may not build new plants for generating electricity. Thus, as the demand for electricity increases, the existing plants may be unable to produce enough power to meet future consumer needs.

Instant Replay

Interest rates are determined by supply and demand, risk, and the rate of inflation.

As interest rates increase, the demand for capital goods decreases.

If businesses do not invest in capital goods, consumers will have fewer goods and services in the future.

MEETING THE MONEY NEEDS OF BUSINESSES

Businesses need money for many reasons. A new company may require money to get started. An existing business could spend millions or even billions of dollars to expand into new areas or products. An unprofitable business may be forced to find financial help just to continue in business.

Sometimes a business may be able to meet its money needs from the profits it earns. Often, however, money must come from other sources. Corporations commonly sell bonds or stocks to obtain the extra dollars they need.

Bonds

A *bond* is a printed promise to repay a certain amount of money, at a certain interest rate, at a certain time. Bonds are sold by corporations, by the federal government, and by state and local governments.

Bonds are usually printed in $1,000 amounts and the repayment is due in 20 or 30 years. The interest rate on the bond is determined by the same three factors described earlier: supply

Illus. 9-3 *Corporations sell stocks and bonds to obtain additional money.*

Chicago Mercantile Exchange

and demand, risk, and inflation. A company may attempt to sell as many $1,000 bonds as necessary to raise needed money. For example, if $1 million is to be borrowed, the company would sell 1,000 bonds.

The bonds sold by corporations can be purchased by individuals. A person who owns a bond is referred to as a ***bondholder***. By buying the bond, the bondholder is lending money to the firm. The bondholder receives the interest that is earned by the bond each year. When the bond is due for repayment, the $1,000 amount of the bond is also repaid to the bondholder.

Stocks

Chapter 6 explains that owners of a corporation are called its ***stockholders***. For a new corporation, the stockholders are those who use their money to get the business started. Often, managers find that an existing company needs more money. They may decide to sell additional shares of stock. Those persons who buy this stock are providing money to be used by the business. In return, they receive part ownership in the business.

An individual's ownership in a corporation is determined by the proportion of all the shares of stock owned. For example, suppose Mr. and Mrs. Lopez own 100,000 shares of stock in an oil company. If the corporation has sold a total of 1 million shares of stock, they own 10 percent of the company.

Dividends. Unlike bondholders, a stockholder does not get guaranteed interest income. Stockholders also do not get their money back after a stated time. The stockholder's reward is the dividend paid by the corporation to its owners. A *dividend* is a portion of the corporation's profits that management sets aside for the stockholders.

For example, management may decide to pay a dividend of $1 per share. This means that the stockholders will receive $1 for each share of stock they own. The owner of 10,000 shares would receive $10,000, while the owner of a single share would receive a check for $1.

The dividend paid to stockholders can change depending on the fortunes of the company. If the company earns a large profit, management may decide to increase the dividend to $1.25 per share. However, if the company does poorly, the dividend might be reduced to 75 cents per share. In a particularly bad year, the company might not pay any dividend at all.

The Stock Exchange

The owners of a firm's stock can sell their shares to other people. The buying and selling of stock usually takes place on a stock exchange. A *stock exchange* is a market where buyers and sellers trade or exchange shares of stock. Although there are stock exchanges in a number of cities, most stocks are bought and sold on either the New York Stock Exchange or the American Stock Exchange. Both are located in New York City.

When people want to buy or sell stock they usually call a *stockbroker*. For example, suppose you want to sell 100 shares of General Motors stock that you own. You would call your broker and relay this instruction. Using a computer, the broker would send the "sell" order to a stock exchange. Another stockbroker may have received instructions from a customer to buy General Motors stock. This information would also be sent to the stock exchange. Those who work at the exchange have the responsibility for making the trade between you and the buyer.

The price at which stockholders are able to sell their stock is determined by supply and demand. If buyers believe that General Motors is going to do well, they will bid up the price of the stock. They do this hoping to profit from dividends or by selling the stock when the price increases. On the other hand, if they don't see a bright future for the company, they will not buy. Or, they will buy only at lower prices.

A stockholder who is able to sell stock for more than his or her original purchase price earns a capital gain. A *capital gain* is a profit from the increase in the price of the stock. Often the chance of a capital gain is more important to a buyer than the dividend currently being paid on the stock.

Differences Between Stocks and Bonds

Bondholders have the first claim to a company's profits. This means that the interest due to bondholders must be paid before any dividends can be paid to stockholders. If the money available is just enough to cover interest to bondholders, no dividend can be paid to stockholders.

On the other hand, bondholders will never receive more money than the amount of interest printed on their bonds. Even if the company earns a large profit, the interest paid to bondholders remains unchanged.

Bonds are less risky than stocks. A bondholder will never receive more than the stated amount of interest. However, unless the company does very poorly, income will never be less than that amount. The reward to the stockholder is less certain. Stockholders take a chance on dividend increases and on capital gains.

Another difference between stocks and bonds is that, as owners, stockholders elect the corporation's board of directors. Bondholders are lenders, not owners. As such, they have no voice in the operation of the company.

Instant Replay

A bond is a printed promise to repay a certain amount of money, at a certain interest rate, and at a certain time.

People buy stock to obtain the dividend and in the hope of earning capital gains when they sell the stock.

Stockbrokers buy and sell stocks on stock exchanges.

Bondholders have the first claim to a company's profits, but they do not vote for the firm's board of directors.

PRINCIPLES OF EFFICIENT PRODUCTION

Businesses bring together factors of production (land, capital, and labor) and organize them to produce goods and services. Because the goal of business is to earn a profit, managers try to get more output from these factors. Improvements are always being made in the way goods and services are produced. As a result, more is produced and the costs of production often are lower.

The production systems in the United States and in other industrial countries such as Japan, Germany, and England have special characteristics. These are discussed here.

Specialization of Labor

Imagine the cost and difficulty of building a car if you had to do it yourself. Suppose you could buy the parts but had to assemble them yourself. It would be a very difficult job for most people. What if you had to make each part as well? This task would be almost impossible. Clearly, if you were asked to make one part rather than the entire car, the task would be easier.

In making cars, one worker makes the doors, another the fenders, and yet another the steering wheel. Other workers assemble the parts. By breaking up the job into smaller parts and assigning workers to specific tasks, each worker can concentrate on making only one thing. This technique is called *specialization of labor*.

Consider the workers who make automobile mufflers. Because all they do is make mufflers, they become very good at this task. Each worker can produce many more mufflers each day than could ten workers who each produced five different auto parts. By concentrating only on mufflers, the workers will find new and better ways to make them.

Think about the people you see at work. Most of them are specialists. Secretaries concentrate on typing letters and reports, machine operators usually run the same machine each day, bricklayers lay bricks, and electricians do wiring. The economy consists primarily of workers who specialize in doing a few things very well. The advantage is greater production.

However, there are some disadvantages to specialization. Sometimes the jobs are so routine that they are boring and offer little job satisfaction. Some workers who know how to do only one small task have difficulty finding new jobs. Also, it is difficult for some workers to see their contribution when they are only performing one small task.

Economics of Work

Mass Production

Closely related to the idea of specialized labor is the concept of mass production. *Mass production* refers to producing goods and services in large quantities using specialized labor. Recall your last visit to a fast-food restaurant. These businesses make large quantities of hamburgers and other food products very efficiently. They can serve large numbers of people very quickly and at relatively low cost. In contrast, a fancy restaurant does not use mass-production techniques. Each meal is cooked to order and served to customers at their table. Of course, this is more costly, and consumers have to pay higher prices.

Many firms use an assembly line as their mass-production method. An *assembly line* usually has a number of people working alongside a conveyor belt that moves the product from one worker to another. Each worker performs one or a few operations on the product, such as driving a few screws, spray painting the item, or perhaps inspecting to see that earlier operations were done correctly.

Most people are familiar with an automobile assembly line. At one end of the factory, workers place a frame on the conveyor belt. As the process continues, workers add wheels, tires, fenders, seats, radios, etc. Usually each worker specializes in one of these operations. A finished car comes off the end of the line. The production of automobiles is very efficient because of the use of mass-production techniques and the specialization of labor.

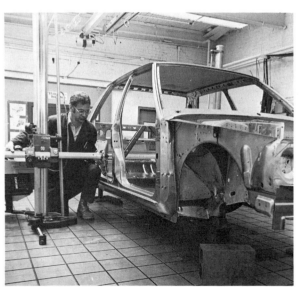

Ford Motor Co.

American Motors Corporation

Illus. 9-4 *Since the time of Henry Ford, the use of mass-production techniques and the specialization of labor has made automobile manufacturing more efficient.*

Capital Goods and Automation

As you remember, capital goods include machinery, tools, vehicles, and most of the things that people use to help them get their work done better and faster. Construction workers almost always use capital goods. These range from hammers and saws to bulldozers and cranes. Secretaries in an office use typewriters, computers, and copying machines. Imagine how difficult it would be to do these jobs without these machines.

One of the most important reasons for the growth of the United States economy has been the development of new and better capital equipment. A business that does not have up-to-date capital equipment may have difficulty staying in business. Its competitors will be able to produce more goods and sell them at lower prices.

Illus. 9-5 *Capital goods such as farm machinery help people get their work done faster and better.*

Courtesy Deere & Co., Moline, IL

Automation refers to the replacement of human labor by machines. In most modern economies, the process of producing goods has been automated. For example, power saws have replaced hand saws on construction jobs; bulldozers have replaced workers with shovels on earth-moving projects; and word processors have replaced typewriters in the office.

A recent automation trend is the use of robots to replace workers on some assembly lines. These robots are machines that do jobs previously done by human labor. They have certain advantages. They tend to be faster, make fewer mistakes, and rarely complain. On some assembly lines, workers do little but watch the product go by. They need only make sure that the capital equipment is running smoothly. Because machines have taken over some of the most routine and repetitive jobs, some workers can be switched to other more interesting jobs.

In some cases, however, the use of robots and other forms of automation has resulted in workers losing their jobs. While this poses problems for those workers, the economy benefits from greater production. Usually workers who lose their jobs in one industry are able to switch to jobs in other fields, although sometimes the adjustment is difficult.

Interdependence

The result of a production system that depends on mass production, specialization of labor, capital goods, and automation is a high degree of interdependence. *Interdependence* means that both workers and businesses are very dependent on one another. For example, if one worker on an assembly line makes a mistake, the entire line may have to be shut down. The result is that the other workers will have to stop work until the error is corrected.

Also, each business in the production process may be very dependent on other businesses. The automobile manufacturer depends on the tire maker to have tires ready to be put on the cars at the right time. If the tires are late in arriving, the production process may stop until they arrive. Occasionally a labor strike in one industry will result in the closing of other industries. For example, a strike in a glass industry can result in the auto plant having to close. If no glass windshields are available, no cars can be finished. Sometimes, a business will build a large inventory of a product needed in its production process if it looks like there may be a strike at one of its suppliers. For example, electric power plants often stock-pile coal if it appears there may be a strike in the coal-mining industry.

Instant Replay

Mass production and the specialization of labor are important reasons for the high standard of living in the United States and some other countries.

The use of machinery and other capital goods to automate the production process is another important part of the United States' production system.

Mass production, specialization, and automation have resulted in an economic system where workers and businesses are very dependent on each other.

SUMMARY

Interest rates are the price of borrowing money. These rates are determined by supply and demand, risk, and inflation. High interest rates reduce the demand for capital goods. Fewer capital goods purchased today mean fewer goods and services for consumers in the future.

Managers often meet their companies' money needs by selling stocks and bonds. A bond is a printed promise to repay a certain amount of money, at a certain interest rate, at a certain time. Stockholders are the owners of a corporation. The owners of stock may receive a dividend. However, the amount of the dividend depends on the profits earned.

Stocks are bought and sold on a stock exchange. The price of a share of stock depends on people's views about how the firm will do in the future. If stockholders sell stock for more than the purchase price, they have made a capital gain.

Stocks and bonds are different in that the bondholder is guaranteed a certain amount of interest each year. In contrast, the stockholder's dividend depends on the amount of profit earned by the firm.

Businesses always try to improve the methods and equipment used to produce goods and services. Specialization of labor, mass production, use of capital goods, and automation are reasons why the economy of the United States and other industrial countries are so productive. In such economic systems, businesses and workers are very dependent on one another.

mass production
assembly line
automation
interdependence
specialization of
   labor
capital gain
bond
dividend
bondholder
stock exchange
stockbroker

In the blank space, write the term that correctly completes the sentence.

1. The use of machines and other equipment to do work previously done by labor is called _____.

2. When the value of common stock increases, the stockholder has received a _____.

3. _____ occurs when workers and businesses must rely on one another.

4. A person who owns one or more bonds is called a _____.

5. The production of goods and services in large quantities using specialized labor is called _____.

6. _____ occurs when workers perform specific tasks in the production process.

7. A _____ is that part of a corporation's profits that is set aside for payment to the stockholders.

8. An _____ consists of a product moving along a conveyor belt with individual workers performing only one or two operations on the product.

9. A _____ buys and sells stock.

10. A _____ is a promise to repay a certain amount of money.

11. The place where stocks and bonds are traded is called a _____.

REVIEW QUESTIONS

1. What three factors determine the interest rate?
2. Which involves more risk, being a stockholder or being a bondholder? Explain.
3. How does the amount of capital goods that businesses purchase today affect the goods and services available to consumers in the future?
4. What are the two ways that stockholders are rewarded?
5. How does specialization of labor reduce the cost of goods and services?
6. Give an example of how automation has reduced costs in the automobile industry.
7. Are there any disadvantages to specialization of labor and the use of assembly lines? Explain.

10

Marketing Goods and Services

The codfish lays ten thousand eggs,
The homely hen but one.
The codfish never cackles
To tell the world she's done.
And so we scorn the codfish,
While the humble hen we prize,
Which only goes to show you
That it pays to *advertise*.

— Anonymous

PREVIEW

Consumers satisfy their needs and wants by purchasing the goods and services produced by businesses. But there must be some link between producers and consumers. This link is called marketing. **Marketing** refers to all the activities involved in getting goods and services from the producer to the consumer. For example, businesses advertise to make people aware of their products. This information helps consumers decide what to buy. Thus, because advertising links the producer and the consumer, it is considered a marketing activity.

In this chapter you will learn about marketing. When you have completed the reading and the learning activities, you should be able to:
• Discuss the importance of marketing in the modern economic system.
• List seven functions of marketing.

130

- Define what is meant by a wholesaler, an agent, and a retailer.
- Discuss four channels of distribution.
- Explain the meaning of form, place, time, and possession utility.

IMPORTANCE OF MARKETING

Marketing activities become more important as economic systems become more complex. In a simple economic system marketing may not play a large role. Think about a small village where the baker makes his or her own flour using wheat purchased from a nearby farm. Orders for pies and cookies are received from people in the village. In such a setting, the baker would have little problem deciding what to bake, and customers would find it easy to complain if the baked goods were not tasty. In this simple economy the link between the bakery and its customers is very close. Marketing activities are not needed because producers and consumers deal directly with one another.

In our modern economic system producers and consumers may not be so closely linked. Large bakeries buy supplies and equipment from many other businesses. They ship pies, cookies, and other baked goods to stores in many cities. The owners of these large bakeries probably never meet the people who buy their products. In this situation, many people form the link between consumers and producers. Truckers move the goods to the grocery stores. People at an advertising agency prepare the ads that are carried in local newspapers and on television and radio. Employees of the grocery store display the baked goods to make them appealing to shoppers. These are all marketing activities.

Today, one-third of all workers in the United States are involved in some form of marketing. Fifty cents of each dollar spent by consumers pays for marketing costs.

Dollars spent on marketing are the price that consumers pay for choice and convenience. Marketing activities provide consumers with a wide variety of goods and services. Individuals can choose between many brands and styles of clothes, stereos, sporting goods, and other merchandise. Marketing brings products to the consumer for convenient shopping. In a large mall a person may be able to find most items on even the longest shopping list. Marketing informs consumers about new products and good buys. Ads in the local newspaper point to the lowest prices on soft drinks, coats, and school supplies. Cutting back on marketing activities certainly could reduce prices, but it would also result in consumers having less information and a smaller variety of goods and services from which to choose.

Illus. 10-1 *Marketing activities are important for large companies.*

MARKETING FUNCTIONS

You have already learned that marketing involves many different activities. However, it is possible to group these activities into seven basic functions:
- Buying
- Grading and Standardizing
- Storing
- Transporting
- Risk-taking
- Financing
- Selling

This section discusses these seven functions using the example of beef moving from producer to consumer.

Buying

Beef cattle are raised on more than 100,000 farms and ranches in the United States. When the cattle have gained enough weight, they are bought by meat packers. As buyers, meat packers perform an important service. Because they purchase large numbers of animals, ranchers are freed from the need to search out individual buyers for their cattle. In effect, meat packers act as collectors, gathering up beef cattle from many locations and bringing them together where they can be efficiently processed.

Grading and Standardizing

Grading and standardizing help the consumer to know the type and quality of goods and services purchased. With beef, the meat packer performs this task. Beef cattle are slaughtered and cut into steaks, roasts, ribs, and other meat cuts. Because of standardization, the consumer knows exactly what is meant by a T-bone steak or a rump roast. Each of these cuts of meat is taken from a specific location on the carcass. For example, when you eat a T-bone steak, you know that the meat comes from the loin of the beef carcass.

Grading tells the consumer the quality of the meat being bought. The United States Department of Agriculture has established a grading system for beef. *Prime* is a term that can be used to describe only the very best beef. Beef that cannot meet the requirements for prime is labeled as *choice*, *good*, or the lowest grade, *standard*. Shoppers know that standard beef is likely to be tougher and less flavorful than the prime grade.

Storing

The local supermarket keeps only enough beef on hand to meet customer needs for two or three days. However, the meat packer stores beef and delivers it to the supermarket as needed.

Storage is also important for other goods. For example, the best time for selling skis is in the fall. If you live in a cold climate

Illus. 10-2 *Many different activities are required to get beef from the producer to the consumer.*

you may have noticed that sporting goods stores begin to increase the size of their ski departments around Labor Day. But ski manufacturers continue to produce skis throughout the year, storing them until they are needed by sporting goods stores.

Transporting

Meat packers buy meat from many sources and locations. Later, the cuts of beef must be delivered to the stores that will sell them to the consumers. Transportation of goods is an important activity in the economic system. Much of what is purchased has been produced hundreds or even thousands of miles away. Without an efficient transportation system, store shelves would quickly become bare. Trucks and railroads are the most important methods of transportation. A ton-mile is a ton of freight moved one mile. Trucks in the United States carried over 500 billion ton-miles of goods in a recent year, while nearly 1,000 billion ton-miles were transported by the railroads.

Risk-taking

Cattle producers, meat packers, and grocery store owners all take risks in selling beef. Producers may be unable to earn a profit because of low beef prices. Packers may suffer a loss because of flood or theft. A power failure could cause the refrigerated beef bought by a grocer to spoil. Although no businessperson enjoys risk-taking, it is a necessary part of doing business.

Financing

If a business stores its product rather than selling it immediately, it may need money to pay its bills. Financing refers to obtaining funds to meet the money needs of the business during these periods. Stocks and bonds are among the sources of such funds. A business may also get funds by borrowing money from a bank. In some cases, a company from which the business bought goods or services may be willing to wait for its money. A seller who does not require immediate payment is said to have extended *credit* to the buyer.

Selling

The grocery store sells beef and other products to consumers. But selling involves much more than just the exchange of goods and services. The grocery store must provide the customer with a convenient and pleasant place to shop. Many stores have gone out of business because they had a poor location or because their poor appearance scared away customers. In contrast, other stores have increased their sales by playing pleasant music and decorating the building in an attractive manner.

Selling also involves packaging and displaying goods in an appealing way. Meats are enclosed in clear wrappings that keep them fresh and allow customers to see how the meat looks. Free samples are provided to encourage people to try new products. Candy, cigarettes, and magazines are placed next to check-out counters in the hope that shoppers will decide to buy them while waiting in line.

A very important part of the selling effort is advertising. *Advertising* refers to paid messages that are designed to make consumers aware of a product and to encourage them to buy it.

Instant Replay

Marketing is the link between producers and consumers.

Dollars spent on marketing are the price that consumers pay for choice and convenience.

Seven marketing activities are buying, standardizing and grading, storing, transporting, risk-taking, financing, and selling.

CHANNELS OF DISTRIBUTION

Once a good is produced, the firm must decide how to market it. Some products are sold directly to the consumer. An example is fresh vegetables purchased from a roadside market. This is called direct marketing. Other products pass through various businesses on their way to the consumer. This is called indirect marketing. The path that goods take as they move from the original producer to the final consumer is called the *channel of distribution*.

Businesses involved in marketing activities are called *intermediaries*. In general, intermediaries link the producer with the consumer. Three important types of intermediaries are agents, wholesalers, and retailers.

Agents

Agents buy and sell for others. They do not actually purchase goods and services. Rather, they arrange for transfers between owners and buyers. A stockbroker is an example of an agent. She or he does not buy stock. The broker simply sends the buyer's order to the stock exchange. Another broker sends the seller's order to the stock exchange. Those who work at the exchange match the orders of buyers and sellers.

Wholesalers

Wholesalers buy goods in large quantities from farmers, manufacturers, and other wholesalers. These goods are then sold to others who, in turn, resell them to consumers. Wholesalers are specialists. By buying large amounts of a small number of goods, they are able to purchase goods at lower prices. Also, because the wholesaler repeatedly buys the same goods, he or she becomes an expert in judging the quality of the products. The benefits of low prices and good judgment can then be passed on to the wholesaler's customers.

Retailers

Retailers buy goods in order to sell them to consumers. They can be grouped by the type of store and the form of ownership.

Type of Store. Retailers may sell many types of goods or handle only a few lines of merchandise. A department store sells a large variety of goods including furniture, appliances, and clothing. Supermarkets provide a broad selection of food and drug items. Specialty stores concentrate on a few products such as tapes and records or maternity clothes. Mail-order houses sell goods through catalogs. Vending machine operations provide snacks and drinks. However, all these businesses are retailers.

Form of Ownership. Many retail stores are independently owned. Others are part of a large corporate chain. For example, if there is a Penney's or a Sears store in your community, it is part of a chain of hundreds of such stores throughout the country. The franchise is a third type of ownership. A franchise is associated with, but not owned by, its parent company. Many fast-food restaurants are franchises.

Four Channels of Distribution

Although many goods have their own special path from producer to consumer, it is possible to identify four general channels of distribution. They are shown in Figure 10-1. The figure also lists some examples of goods that follow each path.

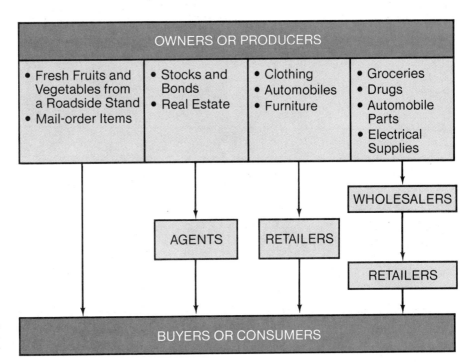

Figure 10-1 *There are four primary channels of distribution for goods.*

Producer to Consumer.   This channel involves goods that are sold directly by the producer to the consumer. When you buy cookies from the local bakery the sale follows this channel. A book purchased by mail from its publisher is another example of this direct form of marketing.

Producer to Agent to Consumer.   The purchase of stocks and bonds uses an agent to transfer ownership from the seller to the buyer. A real estate salesperson also acts as an agent for the seller of a house. She or he tries to find a buyer and then helps to complete the sale.

Producer to Retailer to Consumer.   A grocery store that buys apples from a farmer and sells them to its customers is using this path. The retailer's efforts are useful to the consumer. By performing the various marketing functions, the retailer saves the customer time and expense. The individual consumer does not have to locate the apples, drive out to get them, or check their quality.

Producer to Wholesaler to Retailer to Consumer.   The wholesaler helps the retailer in many of the same ways that the retailer helps the consumer. For example, a grocery store sells

Illus. 10-3 *Some goods are sold directly by the producer to the consumer.*

USDA Photo by David Warren

thousands of different items. It would be very difficult for the managers of the store to find the producers of each good. Wholesalers usually deal in a small number of food items such as canned goods or meats. By specializing, they learn a great deal about these goods. Thus, the retailer relies on the wholesaler to make wise buying decisions and to get the products to the retailer.

Economics of Work

Individuals involved in marketing activities are called intermediaries.

Agents assist buyers and sellers. Wholesalers buy goods and sell them to retailers. Retailers sell goods and services directly to consumers.

Important channels of distribution include (1) producer to consumer, (2) producer to agent to consumer, (3) producer to retailer to consumer, and (4) producer to wholesaler to retailer to consumer.

MARKETING AND THE UTILITY OF GOODS AND SERVICES

Consumers buy goods and services because those items have utility. *Utility* refers to the ability of a good or service to satisfy human needs and wants. The utility of basic resources (land, labor, and capital) is increased by production and marketing activities. In particular, marketing activities can significantly increase the utility of a product. This can be seen by considering four types of utility—form utility, place utility, time utility, and possession utility.

Form Utility

Form utility involves changing the structure or shape of resources in ways that increase their value to consumers. For example, the value of trees can be increased when they are transformed into lumber and paper products. Form utility is added primarily by the production process.

Place Utility

When goods and services are available where they are needed, place utility has been added. Marketing creates place utility by getting products from producers to consumers. An example would be shipping paper products to a school for use by students.

Illus. 10-4 *A musical instrument has utility to a musician.*

Time Utility

Some goods and services are more valuable at one time than at another. For example, snow skis are used in the winter, while water skis are a summertime product. An important part of marketing is to get products to consumers at the time when they have greatest value. When this is accomplished, time utility is increased.

Possession Utility

People differ in the value they place on various goods and services. A baseball player would place high value on a new mitt, but a violinist would prefer a new instrument. Unless goods and services are provided to the right people, resources will be wasted. Possession utility involves getting things to the right consumers. Clearly, this is an important marketing objective.

SUMMARY

Marketing is the link between producers and consumers. It becomes more important as the two groups become separated in a complex economic system. About one-half of the price of goods and services goes for marketing. Seven marketing activities are buying, grading and standardizing, storing, transporting, risk-taking, financing, and selling.

Those involved in marketing activities are called intermediaries. Agents, wholesalers, and retailers are all intermediaries. Agents assist others in buying and selling. Wholesalers buy from producers and resell to retailers. Retailers sell directly to consumers. Channels of distribution can be either direct or indirect. A direct channel would be from producer to consumer. An indirect channel would involve goods flowing from producer to wholesaler to retailer to consumer.

Utility refers to the ability of goods and services to satisfy human needs and wants. Production increases form utility, while marketing increases place, time, and possession utility.

BUILDING YOUR VOCABULARY

credit
agent
channel of
   distribution
retailer
marketing
wholesaler
intermediaries
advertising
utility

In the blank space, write the term that correctly completes the sentence.

1. Individuals involved in marketing are called
   _____.

2. A stockbroker is an example of an _____.

3. A _____ sells directly to consumers.

4. The activities involved in getting goods from producers to consumers are referred to as _____.

5. A _____ buys from producers and sells to retailers.

6. The path goods take between the producer and consumer is called the _____

7. _____ attempts to make consumers aware of a product and to get them to buy it.

8. Sellers who do not require immediate payment have extended _____ to buyers.

9. _____ refers to the ability of a good to satisfy wants and needs.

REVIEW QUESTIONS

1. Why isn't marketing very important in a simple economic system such as a village?

2. Other than by advertising, how can a business encourage people to buy its products?

3. What is the difference between an agent and a wholesaler?

4. What is the difference between a wholesaler and a retailer?

5. What is the difference between direct and indirect marketing?

6. Give an example of how marketing can increase place utility.

7. How do consumers benefit by the grading of beef?

11

Business and Society

"No man is an island..."

— *John Donne*

PREVIEW

John Donne's words are even more true today than they were when he wrote them in the seventeenth century. More than ever before, individuals, businesses, and nations depend on one another.

Today, people rely on businesses for most of the goods and services they need and want. Suppose you were allowed to have only those things that you could make by yourself. What would you have to do without? Could you grow enough food for your needs? Do you know how to build a house? What would life be like without Sony to make television sets and Toyota to manufacture cars?

This chapter considers the important role of business in society. It will help you understand why community leaders try to attract businesses to their area. You will also learn about the importance of trade between nations and about rights and responsibilities of business.

When you have completed the reading and the learning activities, you should be able to:

- Explain how a new business in a community can create jobs for the local citizens.
- List some of the problems that can occur when businesses enter or leave a community.

- Explain how the principle of comparative advantage allows trade between nations to benefit the citizens of each country.
- Define the terms *exports* and *imports*.
- List some of the problems created by trade between nations.
- Discuss the rights and responsibilities of business in society.

BUSINESS IN THE COMMUNITY

Most communities have a Chamber of Commerce. Businesses and leading business people usually belong to this organization. Often, one of the Chamber's main objectives is to encourage new businesses to locate in the area. However, some communities are not anxious to attract new businesses. They have decided that the problems created by growth are greater than the benefits. There are both advantages and disadvantages in having new companies locate in a community. The benefits and problems that businesses bring to communities are discussed below.

Advantages

A new business in an area provides jobs, pays taxes, and may improve the quality of life in the community.

New Jobs.   It is important that jobs be available in a community. If people are unable to find employment, they will be forced to leave the area. This is a special concern of young people looking for their first jobs. If no employment is available, they must move to other cities or states. As young people continue to leave, the community becomes smaller and the population becomes older.

A new business will provide jobs for the workers it needs to produce goods and services. In addition, each new business will create employment opportunities beyond its own needs. That is, in addition to persons hired by the company, other jobs are created. For example, a business that hires 100 workers may end up creating a total of 200 new jobs in the community.

To understand this *multiplied effect*, consider what happens when new workers are hired. Suppose these people did not previously have jobs. Once employed, their incomes increase. They will use these extra earnings to buy more goods and services. Many of these goods and services will be purchased from businesses in the community. For example, they will buy food from the local grocery store and gasoline at the corner service station. They are also likely to take in an occasional movie at the drive-in. With their extra dollars, some may even buy a new car from the local car dealer.

Additional jobs also result because companies do business with each other. Over and above the employees hired, the materials and services purchased also create new jobs. The post office may need additional people to pick up and deliver mail. The company will buy paper and other supplies from local dealers, and stationery will be ordered from the local printer. Trucking companies will expand to handle shipments and deliveries. Additional police, fire fighters, and sanitation workers may also be employed by the city. These workers will also spend money in the community—creating still more jobs. In this way, each new business has a multiplied effect on employment in the community.

Taxes. Like individuals, businesses pay taxes. Some of these taxes are paid to local communities in which the businesses are located. For example, cities and states require businesses to pay property taxes. The property tax is based on the value of the property owned by the business. This includes buildings, machinery, and the land owned by the company.

The property taxes paid by a business can be used to pay for schools, parks, street repairs, and other community services. Taxes paid by a large business may total millions of dollars each year. As businesses pay taxes, the tax burden on individual citizens is reduced. Additional information about property taxes and other forms of taxation is presented in Chapter 14.

Improved Quality of Life. Many businesses require workers with special training. Often, a new business will provide this training for its employees. These people develop skills that they would not have learned if the company had not come to the area. Such skills allow workers to earn higher wages and also to improve their future job opportunities.

The opening of a large business can improve the quality of life in a community in other ways. Sometimes a business will donate large amounts of money for parks or other recreational facilities in the town. Many companies set up scholarships that allow deserving students to attend college. Some give their employees time off from work and pay tuition to assist them in getting a college degree.

It is not unusual for the managers of a business to be leaders in civic affairs. When funds must be raised for a hospital or to enlarge the community library, management skills can be useful. In other cases, business leaders may be involved in supporting theater, music, or athletic activities.

Disadvantages

There are some disadvantages in having a new business in a community. These include harm to the environment and a heavy burden on community services. Also, when a business closes or leaves an area, serious problems may be created for the community.

Harm to the Environment. The term *environment* refers to the water, air, vegetation, and other natural surroundings in an area. Some companies have the potential of doing great harm to the environment. For example, a plant that makes paper may cause an unpleasant smell for miles around. A coal-burning electric plant can pollute the air. A nuclear generating plant increases the risk of radiation exposure in an area. The government's role in protecting the environment is discussed in Chapter 13.

Increased Need for Community Services. When a large business comes to a small community, the services needed may be greater than the community can provide. The children of new workers may overcrowd the schools. The local hospital may no longer be large enough. The water and sewer systems may be too small to serve the increased population.

The business and its employees pay taxes. However, the demand for services often increases before the tax payments do. Energy development in the western United States is a good example. Coal mines and electric generating plants near Rock Springs, Wyoming, caused that town's population to double in four years. The community was not able to provide for the needs of its new citizens. The growth in population led to a shortage of housing. The small police force was unable to maintain law and order adequately, and many of the roads were little more than mud ponds. For Rock Springs, the coming of new businesses resulted in serious difficulties.

Risk of Job Losses. A new business has a multiplied effect on creating jobs. So it is not surprising that the closing of a business can have a multiplied effect in reducing job opportunities. When employees lose their jobs, they have less money to spend. This means that less is spent on the goods and services provided by other businesses. As a result, these other companies must let some of their workers go. In total, the number of jobs lost is greater than the number of workers released by the company that closed.

Illus. 11-1 *A business can improve the quality of life in a community by providing scholarships that allow deserving students to attend college.*

Instant Replay

Advantages of a new business locating in a community include a multiplied increase in jobs, additional tax revenues, training for workers, and high-quality leadership.

Disadvantages of a new business include possible harm to the environment, extra demand for community services, and a multiplied loss of jobs if the business fails.

BUSINESS IN THE WORLD

Business activity links the world together. Airlines of many nations fly planes made in the United States. Cattle in the Soviet Union feed on American grain. Oil in the Middle East is produced using drilling equipment made in the United States.

Citizens in this country also benefit from goods provided by other countries. American highways are crowded with Toyotas, Mazdas, and Subarus manufactured in Japan. Millions of gallons of gasoline used by those cars come from Saudi Arabian oil. The

Illus. 11-2 *International trade benefits people in the United States who use petroleum products that come from other nations.*

Marathon Oil Company

coffee that gets some people going in the morning is purchased from countries in South America, such as Colombia. Trade between nations is important in our modern world.

When nations exchange the goods they produce, that activity is called ***international trade***. Trade between nations enables people to have goods they might otherwise have to do without. No country can provide all of the goods and services its citizens want. Thus, some of the items consumed might not be available without international trade.

The Principle of Absolute Advantage

Human, natural, and capital resources are necessary to produce goods and services. But these resources are not distributed equally among nations. Some countries have abundant natural resources but few capital goods. Other countries have plenty of human resources, but few natural resources. International trade

Economics of Work

allows nations to concentrate on the activities for which they are best suited. Countries with many workers can produce goods that require much labor, while countries with valuable natural resources can focus on developing and selling these resources.

When a country can produce a good or service at lower cost than another country, it is said to have an ***absolute advantage***. For example, Colombia, in South America, possesses more than 90 percent of the world's supply of emeralds, a gemstone that exists in small quantities in a few other nations. Thus, Colombia is said to have an absolute advantage in producing emeralds. In contrast, the capital goods owned by automakers in the United States allow vehicles to be produced at a much lower cost than they could be produced in Colombia. Hence, the United States has an absolute advantage in manufacturing cars.

Clearly, countries should specialize in making those goods and services for which they have an absolute advantage. This specialization allows an economic system to operate more efficiently, and it results in the production of more goods and services. A simple example will help you understand this idea. Suppose Country A has few people but many valuable natural resources, such as oil and iron ore. In contrast, suppose country B has a large population but is short on natural resources except for good farmland.

If Country A is not involved in international trade, its citizens may find it difficult to obtain certain goods. There may be plenty of gasoline available, but a lack of skilled workers could limit the number of cars that can be manufactured. This country may also be unable to produce enough food to feed its people because it has few workers and unsuitable land for agriculture.

With its excellent farmland, Country B can produce more food than its people need. This nation also has plenty of workers to manufacture automobiles. But there is not enough iron ore to make steel for automobile parts. Country B also is unable to produce enough gasoline to meet the demands of its citizens.

The Principle of Comparative Advantage

It is not surprising that both trading partners can benefit by specializing in those products for which they have an absolute advantage. But what if one nation is more efficient at producing both of the goods to be traded? For example, suppose that both beef and computers can be produced at lower cost in the United States than in Taiwan. Table 11-1 shows the hypothetical opportunity cost (in terms of American dollars) of producing both of these goods in each country. Note that both a pound of beef and a computer cost less to produce in the United States than in Taiwan. That is, the United States has an absolute advantage in producing both beef and computers. In this situation, is there any reason why the two countries might benefit by trading with each other? The answer involves the concept of **comparative advantage**, which means that a country benefits from specializing in the production of those products at which it is relatively most efficient.

Costs of Producing Beef and Computers in the United States and Taiwan

Country	Beef	Computers
United States	$2 per pound	$500 each
Taiwan	$5 per pound	$750 each

Suppose in this example that beef and computers are the only two goods produced in both Taiwan and the United States. To determine which country has the comparative advantage in producing computers, you have to determine how much it would cost each country—its opportunity cost—to switch its resources from producing beef to making computers. In this case, according to Table 11.1, the United States would have to give up 250 pounds of beef ($500 ÷ $2) to produce one computer. But in Taiwan, the opportunity cost of producing one computer is only 150 pounds of beef ($750 ÷ $5). Therefore, as the opportunity cost is less for Taiwan than the United States, Taiwan would have a comparative advantage in producing computers.

The same principle of comparative advantage holds true for trading as for producing computers and beef between the two countries. Suppose that an importer suggests trading one Taiwanese computer for 200 pounds of American beef. In Taiwan the computer can be traded for only 150 pounds of beef, so this trade is good for the Taiwanese. At the same time, the opportunity cost of providing a computer in the United States would be 250 pounds of beef, but the cost of getting a computer by trading with Taiwan is only 200 pounds of beef. Thus, the trade also benefits people in the United States.

Whenever nations have a comparative advantage, they can benefit from trade even if one of the nations has an absolute advantage in both goods. Each country should specialize in the production of the good for which it has the comparative advantage. Thus, Taiwan will produce computers and the United States will produce beef.

150

Instant Replay

The exchange of goods and services between nations is called international trade.

Even if a country has an absolute advantage in producing all goods, it can benefit from international trade by specializing in those goods for which it has a comparative advantage.

Exports and Imports

The goods that a nation sells to other countries are called *exports*. Goods purchased from other nations are called *imports*. About 10 percent of business activity in the United States deals with exports and imports. This may seem like a small proportion, but the number of workers and dollars is very large. In 1986 businesses in the United States exported $276 billion of goods. In that same year, the value of imports was almost $370 billion. In this country, the jobs of some three to four million people are connected with international trade.

Illus. 11-3 *About 10% of business activity in the United States involves exports and imports.*

The Port Authority of New York and New Jersey

The most important exports of the United States are capital goods and agriculture products. The capital goods include products such as airplanes, computers, and oil drilling equipment. The ability of United States business to produce high-quality capital goods has placed such items in great demand. The vast amount of food produced in America allows this nation to be the world's largest exporter of agricultural products.

Some products are not produced at all in the United States. For example, virtually all of the bananas, cocoa, and natural rubber used in the United States are imported. Large amounts of other resources are also purchased from other countries. Billions of gallons of oil come into the United States each day. Some important metals are obtained almost entirely from other nations. Table 11-2 shows the percentage of certain metals that are imported.

Table 11-2 *This chart shows the percentage of metals used in the United States that are imported from other countries.*

Imports As a Percentage of Total U.S. Consumption of Certain Metals

Metal	Import Percentage
Aluminum Ore	90%
Chrome	90
Gold	54
Nickel	92
Platinum	95
Tin	81

Although its international trade involves many dollars, the United States is much less dependent on such trade than many other nations. For example, about half of all business activity in Hong Kong is tied to exports and imports. The reason is that Hong Kong is a small area and is forced to specialize. Its advantage is human resources. Goods made by workers in Hong Kong can be found all over the world. However, Hong Kong has few natural resources. Thus, fuel, food, and materials for making goods must be imported.

Advantages of International Trade

You have learned that international trade allows people to have goods that would not otherwise be available. Exchange between nations has other advantages as well. One is that competition between businesses may increase. The hand calculator industry is a good example. To avoid losing sales to Japanese manufacturers, American calculator makers have been forced to compete harder. American companies have reduced prices and provided a greater variety of products for sale.

International trade also links nations together in other ways. As businesspersons work together, they come to understand one another. This makes them more tolerant of lifestyles in other nations. Trade also provides a reason for the leaders of nations to cooperate. Countries that depend on the goods of their neighbors are usually more likely to seek peaceful solutions to their differences.

Disadvantages of International Trade

The links created by trade between nations can also cause problems. Sometimes international trade can be used as a weapon to achieve political goals. The oil embargo of the Arab nations in the 1970s is a good example. Oil exports to the United States were cut off. This was an attempt to force the United States to abandon its support of Israel. In 1980, the United States tried to use grain as a weapon against the Soviet Union. Sales of wheat to Russia were cut off as a protest against that nation's invasion of Afghanistan.

Competition resulting from international trade can also cause problems. Japanese manufacturers have captured a large share of the American automobile market. The sales lost by General Motors, Ford, and Chrysler have forced these companies to lay off workers. In communities such as Detroit, where automobile manufacturing is the main business, unemployment has been high. Managers and union leaders in the automobile industry have suggested that the government limit imports to protect American jobs.

One way of limiting competition from imports is through *tariffs*. A tariff is a tax placed on imported goods. The tax increases the price of imports and reduces sales. Although tariffs may protect the jobs of workers, they can create additional problems. First, imported goods become more expensive and less available. Second, tariffs invite retaliation. A tariff on imports into the United States may result in tariffs by other countries on United States exports. Because United States exports would then cost more, fewer would be sold.

Exports are goods sold to other countries. Imports are goods purchased from other countries.

International trade links nations together socially and politically. It also can benefit consumers by increasing competition between firms.

Problems that may result from international trade include its use as a weapon to achieve political goals and the loss of jobs at home.

Tariffs can be used to reduce imports. However, they increase prices paid by consumers and invite retaliation.

RIGHTS AND RESPONSIBILITIES OF BUSINESS IN SOCIETY

In a country such as the United States, businesses have certain rights. However, at the same time, they also have responsibilities that must be met.

Rights of Business

You learned in Chapter 1 that the United States has a mixed economic system in which some decisions are made by government, but most decisions are left to individuals. In this mixed system, business owners usually have the right to decide what they will provide, how to produce it, and how much to charge for it. If the owners of the business make wise choices, they will be rewarded with large profits. Similarly, the employees of the business will earn good salaries and not have to worry about losing their jobs. The right to succeed and to be rewarded for that success is a basic right of business.

However, if business managers select a product that consumers don't like or if they set the price too high, the business may fail. When the business fails, the owners may lose the money they invested and the workers may lose their jobs. Although it is not a very pleasant notion, the right to fail is another basic right of business. Business failures are difficult for those involved, but they free resources for other uses and also provide signals about what customers want and what they are willing to pay.

Illus. 11-4 *Business owners have the right to succeed. If they produce a product that consumers like and will buy, such as this stereo headset, they will be rewarded.*

When the government in a mixed system exercises its right to make decisions, businesses have a right to expect that these decisions be fair. The rules for business activity should be easily understood by everyone, and one firm should not be given an advantage over another. Businesses also have a right to expect that conditions will be favorable for business activity. For example, a prosperous economy requires that people have confidence in the money provided by government and that there be ways to resolve disagreements between individuals.

Business Responsibilities

In an economic system where most decisions are made by individuals, it is important that those decisions be made in a responsible manner. One reason for government involvement in the economic system is the belief that many business decisions are harmful to society.

We live in a fragile environment and are rapidly consuming our scarce natural resources. When a firm pollutes the water or the air, the resulting effect on the environment makes life much less pleasant for others. Similarly, if businesses use scarce natural resources such as oil or coal in a wasteful manner today, future generations may not have enough of these resources. Business has a responsibility to care for the environment and to conserve on the use of scarce natural resources.

Illus. 11-5 *Businesses have a responsibility to make sure their workers perform in a safe environment and use safety equipment such as goggles for a welder.*

TRW Inc.

Business also has a responsibility to provide useful and safe products to consumers and to make sure that workers perform their tasks in a safe workplace. In a market economy, there are forces that cause this to happen. Consumers will refuse to buy poor-quality products, and workers will not work in locations that appear to be unsafe. But consumers cannot always be sure which products are shoddy, and a worker may not be aware of a dangerous situation until she or he is injured.

In a large and complicated economic system there will always be those who behave in an irresponsible manner. As a result, government may have to step in to assure responsible behavior. The role of government in the economic system is discussed in Chapter 13.

SUMMARY

A new business provides more new jobs than the actual number of workers hired by the company moving into a community. Businesses also pay taxes that can be used to provide community services. A third benefit of business is the possible improvement in the quality of life in the area.

A business closure may have multiplied effect on job losses in a community. Some businesses can harm the environment. A large business coming into a small town may require more community services than the area can provide.

The exchange of goods and services between nations is called international trade. A country has an absolute advantage when it can produce a product more efficiently than another country. A comparative advantage exists when the opportunity cost of a product in terms of other goods is less than in other countries. International trade causes the economic system to operate more efficiently by encouraging nations to specialize in those products for which they have an absolute or comparative advantage.

Goods sold to other countries are called exports. Goods bought from other nations are called imports. The United States exports capital goods and agricultural products and imports natural resources such as oil and metals.

International trade helps people understand other ways of life. However, it can also be used as a weapon to achieve political goals. Trade between nations increases competition in selling goods. This can also result in a loss of jobs in some industries. Tariffs are taxes on imports that tend to reduce the amount of international trade.

Businesses have a right to succeed and to fail. They also have a right to expect that decisions made by government will be fair. Businesses have a responsibility to protect the environment, conserve on the use of scarce resources, and provide safe products and workplaces.

BUILDING YOUR VOCABULARY

environment
exports
tariff
comparative
   advantage
absolute advantage
international trade
imports
multiplied effect

In the blank space, write the term that correctly completes the sentence.

1. When goods and services produced in different countries are exchanged, that activity is called _____.

2. Goods sold to other countries are _____.

3. A tax placed on certain imports is called a _____.

4. A new business in a community has a _____ by causing new jobs to be created in other businesses.

5. When a country can provide a product at a lower cost than another country, it is said to have an _____.

6. The ability to provide a product relatively more efficiently than another country is called _____.

7. Goods purchased from other countries are _____.

8. The water, air, vegetation, and other surroundings in an area constitute the _____.

REVIEW QUESTIONS

1. How can a new business in a community have a multiplied effect on the number of jobs?
2. What are some of the ways in which business can improve the quality of life in an area?
3. What are some of the problems that could result when a large business moves into a small town?
4. Why does international trade allow the citizens of nations to be better off than if there were no trade?
5. Why is a country like Hong Kong more involved in international trade than the United States?
6. List the major exports and the most important imports of the United States.
7. How does international trade increase competition? What problem may be created by increased competition?
8. What would happen if the government intervened and prevented firms from failing?

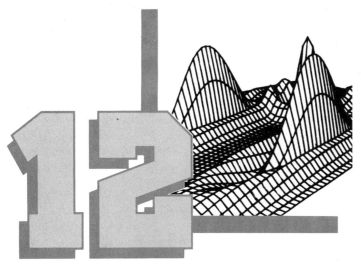

Economic Barometers: Grading the System

PREVIEW

It is useful to have measures of the performance of individual players on a basketball team. A team's outstanding players are usually judged on the basis of their statistics. These include scoring average, rebounds per game, field goal percentage, free throw percentage, and assists.

Measuring the performance of the economic system is also useful. Good measures allow problems to be identified that may require government attention. This chapter considers various measures of the performance of the economic system.

When you have completed the reading and the learning activities, you will be able to:
- Identify the gainers and losers from inflation and explain how the rate of inflation is measured.
- Discuss what is meant by Gross National Product and per capita income and how these measures are used to evaluate the economic system.
- Explain how the rate of unemployment is measured.
- List the four phases of the business cycle.
- Explain what is meant by the balance of trade.

INFLATION AND DEFLATION

Inflation occurs when the prices of many goods, services, and resources are increasing. Inflation means to blow up, or increase in size. During inflation, the costs of goods and services that people need and want increase. Thus, during a period of inflation, people's dollars buy less than they did in the past. For example, the same goods and services that could have been purchased for $100 in 1970 would have cost $340 in 1987. In the United States, the general level of prices has increased each year since 1950.

Inflation in other nations has sometimes been much more rapid than the recent experience in the United States. After World War I, the leaders of Germany tried to pay that country's war debts by turning on the presses and printing money. The result was a very high rate of inflation. A sandwich that cost the equivalent of $1.00 on July 1, 1922, would have been over $4,000 on New Year's Day, 1923.

Rapid inflation in Germany caused people to lose confidence in that nation's money. Merchants refused to accept marks (the German currency) as payment for goods and services. For some time, barter was the main method of exchange. To restore confidence in the use of money, a new kind of money based on gold was issued. The old marks could be traded for the new ones. However, it took one trillion (1,000,000,000,000) of the old to get just one of the new gold marks. As people gained confidence in the new money, the use of barter gradually disappeared.

Deflation is defined as a decrease in the overall price of a market basket of goods and services. Although the economy in the United States has generally experienced inflation rather than deflation, there have been some periods when prices have declined. Perhaps the most notable case occurred during the Great Depression. Between 1929 and 1933, prices declined about 25 percent.

GAINERS AND LOSERS FROM INFLATION

Suppose everyone knew the prices of all goods and services were going to double during the next year. Suppose people also knew their incomes were going to be exactly doubled over the same period. Would inflation be a problem? Not really. Each person would have enough money to buy exactly the same goods and services as before the price increase. The increase in prices would be exactly matched by the increased incomes. Also, because people knew about the changes in prices and incomes, no one would be unprepared.

In the real world, one problem created by inflation is that individual income changes do not exactly match price changes. The incomes of some people may increase more rapidly than the rate of inflation. Such people will be better off than before the change in prices.

However, the incomes of other people may not grow as fast as the increase in prices. These people will be worse off because of inflation. They will be able to buy fewer goods and services than before. The gainers and losers from inflation are determined primarily by changes in income in comparison to changes in price. Two groups are particularly likely to be hurt by inflation:
- The elderly
- Creditors

Illus. 12-1 *People with fixed incomes may be caught in a trap during periods of rapid inflation.*

The Elderly.   Certain people live on relatively fixed incomes. This means that the amount of money they have to spend does not change much each year. Elderly people who are retired are especially likely to be in this category. During their working years, individuals put away money to meet the needs of old age. Usually, the amount that is saved is determined by how much people expect they will need in the future. During times of inflation, this retirement fund may not be enough. If the retired person is ill, going back to work to earn more money may not be possible. Without extra help from the government, elderly people often face great difficulties during times of inflation.

Creditors.   *Creditors* are people who lend money. *Debtors* are borrowers of money. Inflation tends to hurt creditors and help debtors. Suppose you borrow $1,000 from the bank and agree to pay it back with interest five years later. During the five years, prices double. The $1,000 that the bank receives back will buy only half as many goods and services as the $1,000 originally lent.

During inflation, debtors benefit by being able to repay their loans with less valuable dollars. However, if creditors expect inflation to occur, they can protect themselves by charging higher interest rates. This extra interest received is payment for the less valuable dollars that will be repaid.

The case of creditors and debtors illustrates another very important effect of inflation. It matters a great deal whether inflation comes as a surprise or whether it is widely expected. People can plan for expected increases in prices. The higher interest rates charged by creditors is one example. Working people saving extra money for retirement is another illustration. An electric company signing a contract to buy coal at a fixed price for many years is another example of inflation planning. If inflationary problems are expected, the results will usually be less serious than if inflation were not expected.

Causes of Inflation

In discussing some of the causes of inflation, two types are covered:
- Demand-pull inflation
- Cost-push inflation

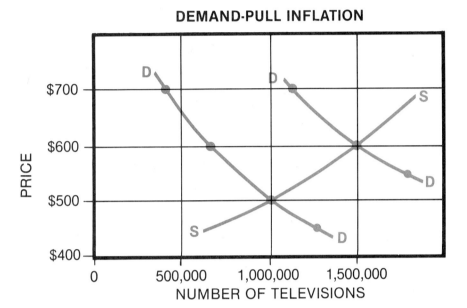

DEMAND-PULL INFLATION

Figure 12-1 *This shows the supply and demand curves for television sets. Increased demand, indicated by the D' curve, raises the market price, creating a demand-pull inflation.*

Demand-Pull Inflation. Chapter 4 describes how the market price is determined by supply and demand. Figure 12-1 shows supply and demand curves for television sets. The demand curve, marked DD, and the supply curve, marked SS, cross where the price is $500. This is the market price of television sets.

Now suppose more people want to buy television sets than before. Perhaps more football games are being shown, or maybe the networks are advertising better movies for the coming year. The increased demand for television sets is shown by the new demand curve, marked D'D'. It indicates that, at each price, more people want to buy television sets than before.

The new demand curve and the supply curve cross at a price of $600. This is the new market price. Note that it is a higher market price than before. That is, an increase in the demand for televisions has pulled up the market price.

Now suppose the demand for many goods and services increases. This could happen because more people are in the economic system or because individuals have more money to spend. Just as with the television set example, the increase in demand causes the prices of these goods and services to increase. This situation is referred to as *demand-pull inflation*. It is sometimes described as too much money chasing too few goods and services.

Cost-Push Inflation. The prices of goods and services are influenced by the costs of producing them. When costs go up, so do prices. In the 1970s, the price of oil went from about $3 a barrel to $30 a barrel. As a result, the price of gasoline, heating oil, and other products using oil increased rapidly. People in the economic system soon realized their incomes were not keeping up with the price changes. Many workers demanded and got higher wages. These higher wages increased the costs for producing goods and services. Thus, businesses had to increase prices even further. When prices are pushed higher by increasing costs, this is called *cost-push inflation*. It is also sometimes referred to as a *wage-price spiral*.

Measuring the Rate of Inflation

Each month, the federal government reports the rate of inflation in the United States for the previous month. The measure of price changes used by the government is called the *Consumer Price Index*.

A problem with measuring the rate of inflation is that the prices of individual goods and services change by different amounts. Although the price of oil went up during the 1970s, the price of handheld calculators went way down. A useful measure of inflation must take into account these differences.

The Consumer Price Index measures the change in the price of a *market basket* of goods and services. This market basket consists of about 400 items that are purchased by the average consumer. It includes things such as bread, gasoline, rent, hair cuts, and movie tickets.

The government determines the cost of this market basket of goods and services each month. This is done by people who go out and find the prices of each of the 400 items in a number of cities. Changes in cost of the market basket are represented by changes in the Consumer Price Index. For example, suppose the market basket cost $1,000 one year and $1,100 the next year. The Consumer Price Index would show that the rate of inflation was 10 percent. (The new cost of $1,100 is 10 percent higher than the old cost, $1,000.)

Figure 12-2 shows the yearly rates of inflation in the United States from 1970 to 1987. Inflation was a serious problem from 1974 to 1981. In 1980 alone, prices went up by nearly 13 percent. However, in recent years the rate of inflation has been much lower.

164

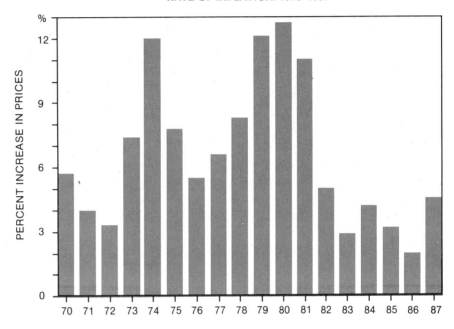

RATE OF INFLATION: 1970–1987

PERCENT INCREASE IN PRICES

Figure 12-2 *Shown here is the rate of inflation for the years from 1970 to 1987.*

Instant Replay

Inflation occurs when the prices of many goods, services, and resources are increasing.

Inflation harms lenders and people living on fixed incomes.

Demand-pull inflation is caused by too much money chasing too few goods. Increases in the cost of producing goods and services may cause cost-push inflation.

Inflation in the United States is measured using the Consumer Price Index.

GROSS NATIONAL PRODUCT AND PER CAPITA INCOME

The performance of a business is often evaluated on the basis of sales during the past year. Sales measure the dollar value of a company's goods and services purchased by consumers, other businesses, and government. If sales are greater than the previous year, a company is usually judged to have done well. However, a decline in sales usually indicates a poor year.

Changes in sales measure the growth of an individual business. It is also important to measure the performance of an entire economic system. If more goods and services are being produced each year, the economic system is said to be growing. This indicates the system may be capable of satisfying additional human wants and needs.

Gross National Product

The most widely used measure of performance of the economic system is the *Gross National Product (GNP)*. Gross National Product measures the dollar value of final goods and services produced in the economic system each year.

Notice that the word "final" appears in the definition. If the dollar value of all goods and services were added up, the result would be misleading. The reason is that some goods and services would be counted more than once. Steel is an example. Suppose the dollar value of all the steel produced was included in GNP.

Remember that steel is used to produce other goods. Automobiles require steel. Steel is an important material used in making typewriters, and it is often found in watches. Cars, typewriters, and watches are all goods produced in the economic system. The prices of these items already reflect the amount of steel needed to make them. Thus, if steel were included in the GNP, it would be counted twice.

To avoid double counting, the Gross National Product includes only final goods and services. "Final" refers to things that are not used as part of some other good or service. Steel, oil, and transistors are not included in counting up the Gross National Product because they are used in other products. In contrast, the dollar values of automobiles, gasoline, and radios are all included because they are final goods. In 1987, the Gross National Product of the United States was more than $4,500 billion.

Inflation creates a problem in measuring the GNP. Suppose the Gross National Product increased by 10 percent in one year. Does that mean that there are 10 percent more goods and services produced than the year before? Not necessarily. Remember, the goods and services used to compute the Gross National Product are measured in terms of their prices. If the rate of inflation was also 10 percent during the year, the GNP change was caused by price increases. The actual or real total of goods and services produced is no greater than the year before.

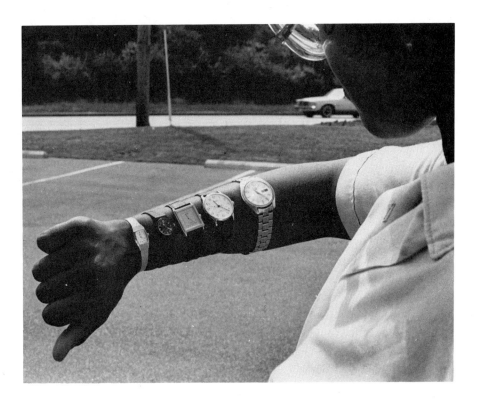

Illus. 12-2 *GNP includes only final goods and services such as watches.*

The effects of inflation on the Gross National Product are eliminated by using a measure called *Real GNP*. Real GNP adjusts for price changes in measuring the amount of goods and services produced. Real GNP is the tool commonly used to measure the growth in the economic system. Suppose newspapers report that Real GNP grew 5 percent over the past year. This means that, after adjusting for inflation, 5 percent more goods and services were produced than the year before.

Per Capita Income

Gross National Product includes the dollars spent by businesses for capital goods and also the purchases made by government. GNP is an important measure of changes in general economic conditions, but it is also useful to examine changes in the incomes received by individuals. The measure used for this purpose is *Per Capita Income*. It is computed by adding up all the income earned by people in the economy (wages and salaries, rent, interest, and profit) and dividing by the number of people.

An increasing Per Capita Income indicates that people have more money with which to buy goods and services. However, when Per Capita Income decreases, this is an indication that people are less well off than before.

Gross National Product is the value of all the final goods and services produced in the economy.

Real GNP adjusts Gross National Product for the effects of inflation.

Per Capita Income is total income earned divided by the number of people.

UNEMPLOYMENT

Unemployment has several causes. In some cases, a person may be unemployed because he or she quit one job to find another. In other situations, lack of skills that are in demand may lead to unemployment.

Unemployment may also result from general conditions in the economic system. Chapter 7 explains that the demand for labor is a derived demand. That is, the demand for goods or services produced by labor determines how many jobs will exist. If the Real GNP declines, fewer goods and services are produced, and fewer workers will be employed. Therefore, unemployment increases when the Real GNP decreases.

Each month the Department of Labor reports the *rate of unemployment* in the United States. The rate of unemployment is the percentage of the total number of workers who cannot find work. The percentage is computed through simple division. The number of unemployed people who want to work is divided by the total of those who are working or want to work.

It would be impossible to contact every person in computing the unemployment rate. In actual practice, about 50,000 people are interviewed each month. The people in this group are selected from all races, places, and occupations.

For a person in the group to be counted as unemployed, he or she must meet three qualifications. First, the person must be at least 16 years old. Second, the individual must be available for work. This means that someone in prison or a person with a broken leg would not be considered unemployed. Finally, the individual must be seeking work. Those who are making no effort to find a job are not counted as unemployed.

Figure 12-3 shows unemployment rates in the United States from 1970 to 1987. These rates are for all categories of workers

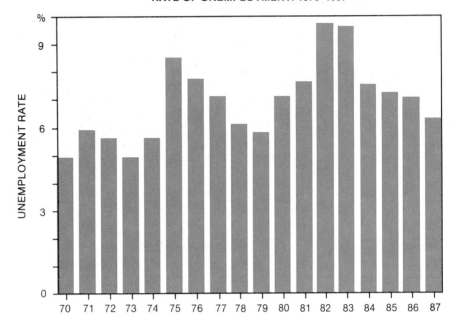

RATE OF UNEMPLOYMENT: 1970–1987

Figure 12-3 *Shown here is the rate of unemployment from 1970 to 1987 for all categories of workers.*

lumped together. The unemployment rates for specific groups can be much different from those shown in Figure 12-3. The group with the highest unemployment rate is usually teenagers. The unemployment percentage for persons between 16 and 19 is often two or three times the rates shown in the figure.

During the 1930s, the rate of unemployment reached 25 percent. This means that one out of four workers could not find a job at that time. The 1930s were a period of economic *depression*. A depression is a time when the Real GNP is falling rapidly, and the rate of unemployment is very high. Mere numbers do not indicate the misery experienced by many families who lived through the 1930s. People lost their homes, their businesses, and their savings. Although few people actually starved, many were uncertain about the source of their next meal.

Economists and politicians sometimes used the term *full employment*. Full employment does not mean that everyone in the United States has a job. There will always be a certain amount of unemployment as people move from one job to another. Full employment is defined as an unemployment rate of 5 or 6 percent. It is usually thought of as a goal for the economy. As you look at Figure 12-3, you will see that in recent years the actual rate of unemployment has been above the full employment rate.

Illus. 12-3 *During the Great Depression of the 1930s, the rate of unemployment reached 25%.*

Instant Replay

The rate of unemployment is computed by dividing the number of people without jobs by the number who are working or want to work.

A depression is a period when GNP is falling and the rate of unemployment is very high.

Full employment is usually considered to be an unemployment rate of 5 or 6 percent.

THE BUSINESS CYCLE

Ideally, economic systems should grow at a smooth, even pace. But in reality, they progress in erratic waves of ups and downs. Each alternating wave of growth and decline in GNP is called a *business cycle*. When an economic system is in the growth part of the cycle, it is said to be in a period of *expansion*; when it is in the downward part of the cycle, it is in *recession*.

Figure 12-4 on page 172 depicts a business cycle graphically. When an economic system is in the expansion phase, GNP, income, and the number of available jobs increase while the

Illus. 12-4 *The growth phase of the business cycle is referred to as an expansion.*

Walgreen Company

unemployment rate decreases. When the expansion phase ends, the economy is at its *peak* and the recession phase begins. Then GNP, income, and the number of available jobs all decrease while unemployment rises. When the recession ends, the economy is at a *trough* and expansion begins again.

No two business cycles are the same, but in our economy the average period of expansion has been about four years, and the average period of recession has been one year. Because expansions are longer than recessions, GNP in the United States has generally been increasing. You can understand this increase better if you think of our economy as a flight of stairs. If you climbed the staircase two steps at a time but fell back one step each time, you would still eventually make it up to the top. In the same way, the nation's economy has grown despite periods of recession.

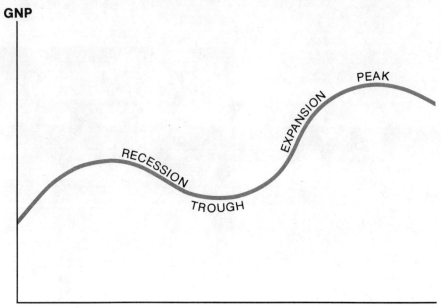

GNP

PEAK

EXPANSION

RECESSION

TROUGH

TIME

Figure 12-4 *The business cycle. The trend in GNP is generally upward, despite periods of decline.*

BALANCE OF TRADE

Thus far, the measures of economic performance that have been discussed involved just the United States. But in Chapter 11 you learned that trade between nations can make everyone better off. Thus, it is important to have measures of international trade. The dollar values of exports and imports are two measures, and a third is the balance of trade.

When a country exports goods, it receives money from other countries. In contrast, imports require that payments be made to other countries. The difference between money received from exports and money spent for imports is called the *balance of trade*. In 1986 imports exceeded exports in the United States by $100 billion. When imports are greater than exports, a country is said to have a negative or unfavorable balance of trade. Economies with an unfavorable balance of trade often experience slower growth than economies with a favorable balance of trade. The balance of trade for the United States has been unfavorable in recent years.

Instant Replay

The business cycle is characterized by alternating periods of expansion and recession.

The dollar value of exports minus imports determines a country's balance of trade.

SUMMARY

Inflation refers to an increase in the prices of many goods, services, and resources. The elderly and creditors are likely to be hurt during periods of inflation.

Demand-pull inflation occurs when there is too much money chasing too few goods and services. Cost-push inflation is the result of increases in the costs of producing goods and services. The rate of inflation in the United States is measured using the Consumer Price Index. This index measures monthly changes in a market basket of items likely to be purchased by individuals.

Gross National Product is defined as the dollar value of final goods and services produced each year. The term *final* means that things such as steel, which are used to produce other goods, are not counted. Inflation may cause year-to-year comparisons of GNP to be misleading. Real GNP is a measure that eliminates the effects of inflation. Per Capita Income is another measure of economic performance. It is computed by dividing total income by the number of people.

The rate of unemployment is defined as the number of people unable to find a job divided by those having or wanting employment. To be counted as unemployed, a person must be at least 16 years old, available for work, and seeking a job.

Periods of expansion followed by periods of recession are called business cycles. A time when GNP is falling rapidly and the rate of unemployment is very high is called a depression.

A nation's balance of trade is computed by subtracting imports from exports. Nations with an unfavorable balance of trade may experience slow growth.

BUILDING YOUR VOCABULARY

inflation
creditor
debtor
recession
rate of
  unemployment
cost-push inflation
balance of trade
depression
peak
trough
Gross National
  Product

In the blank space, write the term that correctly completes the sentence.

1. Too much money chasing too few goods is called _____.

2. An increase in the prices of many goods, services, and resources is referred to as _____.

3. A _____ is a set of goods and services purchased by consumers.

4. A _____ is a period of falling GNP and high unemployment.

5. _____ is a measure that adjusts the value of final goods and services for inflation.

6. The _____ consists of periods of increasing and decreasing GNP.

wage-price spiral
business cycle
market basket
Consumer Price
 Index
demand-pull
 inflation
expansion
deflation
Real GNP
full employment

7. In the _____ phase of a business cycle, GNP is increasing.

8. A person who lends money is called a _____.

9. _____ is occurring when prices of goods, services, and resources are going down.

10. The top of a business cycle is called the _____.

11. _____ measures changes in the dollar value of final goods and services.

12. Inflation is measured using the _____.

13. A _____ is a person who owes money.

14. The low point of a business cycle is called the _____.

15. During the _____ phase of a business cycle GNP is decreasing.

16. _____ occurs when higher costs result in higher prices.

17. Exports minus imports represent a nation's _____.

18. Unemployment divided by those having and looking for jobs is the _____.

19. The _____ is another name for cost-push inflation.

20. If the rate of unemployment is 5 or 6 percent, the economy is said to be at _____.

REVIEW QUESTIONS

1. Why might a debtor be better off as a result of inflation?
2. What is meant by demand-pull inflation?
3. How is a market basket of goods used by the government to measure the rate of inflation?
4. If a country exports $200 billion of goods in a year and imports $150 billion, what would be that nation's balance of trade? Would the balance of trade be favorable or unfavorable?
5. What is the difference between a recession and a depression?

6. List the four phases of the business cycle.

7. Why are only final goods and services included in computing GNP?

8. If the price of automobiles increased by 10 percent each year for the last three years, does this mean that inflation occurred? Why or why not?

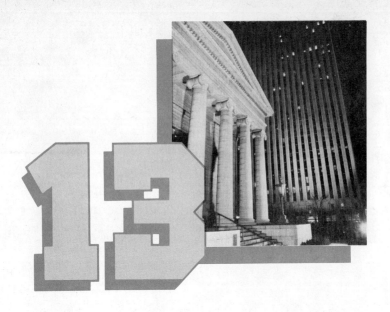

13

Government and the Economic System

PREVIEW

In a free enterprise system, production decisions are determined by consumer demand and by competition among businesses. In a command system, most decisions are made by an individual or a small group associated with the government.

The United States is a mixed economic system. A mixed system leaves most of the decisions about *what to produce*, *how to produce*, and *for whom to produce* to individuals and businesses. However, some economic decisions are made by government. This chapter discusses some of the responsibilities of government in the United States economic system.

When you have completed the reading and the learning activities, you should be able to:

- Explain how government acts as a referee in the economic system.
- Discuss the need for government involvement in the banking system.
- Explain why environmental, worker, and consumer protection are responsibilities of government.
- Discuss how government manages inflation and unemployment in the economy.

GOVERNMENT AS A REFEREE

Imagine being in a boxing match without a referee. You, of course, would fight within the rules. However, if your opponent felt he or she was losing, things could get rough. You could find yourself being gouged, kicked, and bitten. Without a referee to enforce the rules, you would be at a serious disadvantage.

It is equally important to have a referee in the economic system. Someone or some group must have the power to set and enforce rules of fair behavior. Otherwise, people will be forced to spend much of their time and money protecting themselves against unfair practices.

Government acts as a referee in the economic system. Laws are passed stating what individuals and businesses can and cannot do. Once laws are passed, judges, police, and other government officials are responsible for enforcement. Perhaps the best way to illustrate the government's role as a referee in the economic system is with examples.

Theft and Violence

Suppose some "friends" come to your house and steal your car. You politely ask them to return it, but they refuse. At that point, you must either let them keep your car or try to get it back by force. Although you have a right to your car, force is not a good solution. If people tried to solve their problems by force, society would become like a war zone.

One of the responsibilities of government is to protect people from theft and violence. The police will help you get your car back. A judge and jury have the power to decide how to punish the thieves.

Contracts

A contract is a written agreement between at least two people that lists things the people agree to do. For example, the managers of an airline might sign a contract agreeing to buy four airplanes from a manufacturer. Based on the contract, the manufacturer would spend the money necessary to build the planes.

Suppose the airline decides it no longer wants the finished planes. The manufacturer would be left with four unsold airplanes and millions of dollars in bills. Unless there is some way to force the airline to honor the contract, the builder may face serious financial problems.

One of the referee functions of government is to make sure that businesses and individuals live up to their contracts. The

Illus. 13-1 *An airline might sign a contract agreeing to buy airplanes from a manufacturer. One role of government is to make sure that both parties live up to the contract.*

manufacturer could take the airline to court and force the company to honor the contract.

Honest Disagreements

A referee may be necessary to prevent gouging in a boxing match. An example of gouging is when one fighter sticks a thumb in the other's eye. This is clearly against the rules. However, sports referees must also make more difficult decisions. For example, the difference between a blocking foul and a charge in basketball is sometimes very small. Each player may sincerely believe that it was the other who fouled. The role of the referee is to make a fair decision based on what he or she saw.

Honest disagreements also require referees in the economic system. The developer of a video game may believe that another

Economics of Work

company has unfairly copied its game. The second business may argue that their game is different from that of the first company. Each company will use the evidence that best supports its own position. A judge or jury may be needed to make the decision.

Instant Replay

> Government acts as a referee in the economic system by preventing theft and violence, enforcing contracts, and resolving honest disagreements.

GOVERNMENT AS A BANKER

Control of the supply of money is very important in any economic system. The experience of Germany after World War I, described in Chapter 12, is an example. Because so much money was printed, the German mark became worthless. Whenever there is a large increase in the supply of money, its value is likely to decrease.

This example shows that changes in the supply of money can greatly affect the performance of the economic system. In the United States, the job of managing the money supply is given to the *Federal Reserve System*, or the *FED*. The FED is a group of banks with authority to regulate and assist the other banks in the country.

Fractional Reserve Banking

A *bank* is a business that holds money deposited by individuals and other businesses. All banks use *fractional reserve banking*. This means that the amount of money the banks actually have in their vaults is much less than the deposits received. For example, suppose the people in your community had deposited a total of $10,000,000 in the local bank. Now suppose you went to the president of the bank and asked to count all the money in the building. You might find less than $100,000.

What happened to the other $9,900,000? The bank has loaned it out to people who need money. Some of it may have gone to a family that wants to add another bedroom onto its house. Someone may have borrowed money to buy a car. An entrepreneur might have received a loan to start a new business. The bank may also have loaned money to the government in return for government bonds.

How can the bank operate with only $100,000 in its vaults out of the total $10,000,000 in deposits? The answer is that experience has shown that only a very small percentage of depositors want their money at any moment. Therefore, $100,000 should be enough to take care of the day-to-day requirements of depositors.

There is nothing strange about such banking practices. Every bank operates this way. Banks earn their profits from the interest received on loans. If all deposits were kept in the vaults, there would be no money to loan and no profits. The funds kept on hand for the immediate needs of depositors are called **reserves**.

Although fractional reserve banking provides profits for banks and loans for those who need money, it can be risky. Suppose all of a bank's depositors decided they wanted to draw their money out on the same day. After the first $100,000 was given out, the bank's vaults would be empty. The rest of the customers would have to be told that they could not get their money. Imagine how you would feel if you were a latecomer and found out that your life's savings were unavailable.

This can and has happened. In 1907 people began to lose confidence in banks. As a result, they started to withdraw their deposits. Some banks ran out of money. This caused people's confidence in banks to drop even more. More people withdrew their money. Soon, people were frantically running to banks to get their money out. During that year, hundreds of banks were forced to close and thousands of people lost their savings.

Fractional reserve banking works only because people believe that they can get their money when they want it. If there is confidence in the banks, those few who need to make withdrawals can do so without problems. However, if people become worried and make many withdrawals, the banks won't be able to meet the demand for money. At this point, the banking system would cease to work.

Instant Replay

Modern banks keep only a small proportion of total deposits in their vaults at any given time. This is called fractional reserve banking.

Fractional reserve banking works only as long as people have confidence in the banking system.

Economics of Work

Origin of the Federal Reserve System

The bank panic of 1907 made people recognize a need for some control of the banking system. After several years of study, the Federal Reserve System was created in 1913.

The overall responsibility for banking in the United States has been given to the FED's Board of Governors. The *Board of Governors* consists of seven persons. Board members are appointed by the President of the United States and approved by the Senate. They each serve for 14 years. Because money and banking are so vital, FED board members are among the most important people in the entire country. Often, their decisions affect the nation much more than those of any Representative or Senator.

Responsibilities of the Federal Reserve System

The Federal Reserve System is the *central bank* of the United States. This means that it is responsible for the performance of the banking system in this country. Almost every country has some sort of a central bank. No nation leaves banking entirely to private business. Banking and control of the supply of money are too important to be left entirely to individual banks and bankers.

The Federal Reserve System is sometimes called a bank for bankers. It provides some of the same services for banks that those banks provide for individuals and businesses. However, the most important responsibilities of the FED are the following:
- Provide currency to banks.
- Act as a clearinghouse for checks.
- Hold reserves and make loans to member banks.
- Regulate the supply of money.

Provide Currency to Banks. All of the currency used in the United States is printed and distributed by the Federal Reserve System. When paper money becomes worn, a bank can send it back to the FED in exchange for new bills. Each year, the Federal Reserve System shreds millions of dollars of worn paper money.

Act As a Clearinghouse for Checks. Suppose Mr. Cohen buys a new bicycle. He writes a check to be paid by his bank, the First National Bank. The check is deposited in the bicycle shop's bank, the Merchants Bank. At this point, the store has more checkbook money than before, but Mr. Cohen has no less. This is

Federal Reserve Bank—Cleveland Branch

Bureau of Engraving and Printing

Illus. 13-2 *The Federal Reserve System is the central bank of the United States. One of its responsibilities is to provide currency to member banks.*

because the First National Bank does not yet know that he has written the check.

Now the clearinghouse service of the Federal Reserve System comes into play. The Merchants Bank sends the check to the Federal Reserve Bank in its area. The FED then sends the check to the First National Bank, which deducts the amount from Mr. Cohen's account. By having a central clearinghouse, banks don't have to send checks to one another. With some 15,000 banks in operation, this could be extremely complex. Instead, all checks can be cleared through FED clearinghouses.

Hold Reserves and Make Loans to Member Banks. The less money banks hold in their vaults, the more they can loan out. More loans mean more interest and higher income. However, less money in the vault increases potential problems in meeting the withdrawal demands of depositors.

The Federal Reserve System has the power to set the *reserve ratio* for banks. The reserve ratio is the proportion of total deposits that cannot be loaned out. This amount of deposits must be kept in reserve. For example, suppose the reserve ratio is 15 percent. This means the bank must keep on reserve 15 cents out of every dollar deposited.

Not all of this money must be kept in the vaults of the bank. Part can be kept on deposit with the FED. Sometimes a bank may temporarily have too few reserves. One service of the Federal Reserve System is to make loans to help commercial banks during such periods.

Regulate the Supply of Money. The most important responsibility of the Federal Reserve System is to regulate the amount of money in the economic system. The officers of the FED must make sure that there is enough money so that the economy can grow. But it is also necessary to avoid having too much money available. Remember, too much money chasing too few goods causes inflation.

Instant Replay

The Federal Reserve System is the central bank of the United States. It is directed by the Board of Governors.

The FED provides currency to banks and acts as a clearinghouse for checks.

The FED sets the reserve ratio. This ratio is the proportion of deposits that cannot be lent.

The most important function of the FED is controlling the supply of money.

GOVERNMENT AND ENVIRONMENTAL PROTECTION

In producing goods and services, some businesses have done great damage to the environment. Rivers and lakes have become so polluted that neither fish nor people can swim in them. Severe air pollution in some cities prevents residents from seeing the sun. Polluted air has forced some persons to move to protect their health.

Why do businesses often seem unconcerned about damage to the environment? The answer is that a free enterprise system does not reward those who work to preserve natural resources.

The basic objective of a business is to earn a profit. Profits are the difference between dollars received and dollars spent. Thus, if a resource is costly, it can be used sparingly in making a product.

A manager can be less concerned about using resources that are not so expensive. Resources that are free to the company can be used freely.

Air and water are resources used by many businesses in making their products. A steel mill uses the air to get rid of smoke coming from its furnaces. A paper mill may dump waste materials into a river. Because the air and water are free to these businesses, there is no reason to conserve on their use.

Company profits are not affected if the river becomes polluted or if the air is unpleasant to breathe. In fact, any attempt to reduce water and air pollution requires the use of other costly resources. This would cut profits. Thus, the managers normally have no reason to try to protect the environment.

Although profits are not affected by dirty air and water, the quality of life of an area's residents can be greatly affected. It is these residents who are hurt by pollution.

Possibly, the people of the area could threaten not to buy a polluting company's products. However, a business may sell most of its goods to people who live hundreds of miles away. These people would be unaware of the pollution problem. Short of violence, there is no way in a free enterprise system to force companies to change their production methods.

This problem suggests that government needs to step in and protect the environment for present and future generations. Government has the power to make a business account for the cost of its actions. This can be done in a number of ways. First, laws can be passed that prohibit or limit the amount of pollution. Second, the company may be required to buy equipment that reduces the level of pollution. Finally, a business may be forced to pay a fine if it continues to pollute. If the fine is large enough, the company will have a reason to change its behavior.

Government has used all these methods. Clean air laws can force a factory to shut down under certain conditions. Automobiles are required to have pollution-control devices. Fines have been used to punish companies that continue to pollute.

GOVERNMENT AND CONSUMER PROTECTION

The operation of the free enterprise system offers consumers protection against shoddy or unsafe products. Competition forces firms to provide high-quality goods and services. Companies that consistently supply inferior products soon go out of business. In contrast, firms that build a good reputation are likely to do well. However, in some situations government may need to protect the consumer.

Unsafe Products

The federal government protects consumers from unsafe products in a number of ways. In the case of automobiles, the National Highway Traffic Safety Administration requires that all vehicles sold in the United States have certain safety equipment such as shatterproof windshields, adequate headlights, turn signals, padded dashboards, and seat belts. The agency also has the power to require automobile manufacturers to correct problems in vehicles that have already been sold. You probably have read about cars being recalled to have brake, steering, or transmission problems repaired.

The Consumer Product Safety Commission is another federal agency that protects consumers. The commission collects information on injuries caused by various products. This information is used to determine which products are most dangerous. The commission can require that unsafe products be improved or withdrawn from the market.

A recent example involved baby cribs. The commission determined that a number of babies had been injured or killed because their heads became stuck between the slats on the sides of cribs. As a result, an order was issued requiring that the slats be put closer together so that a baby's head could not fit between them.

The Food and Drug Administration performs a similar function. This agency requires that drugs be carefully tested before they are put on the market. Any food or drug that may cause illness or death can be removed from the market by the Food and Drug Administration.

Illus. 13-3 *One way the federal government protects consumers from unsafe products is by requiring warning labels on cigarettes.*

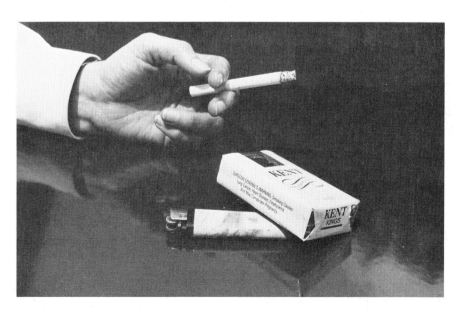

The Food and Drug Administration's insistence on careful, long-term testing has protected American consumers from experiencing the serious side effects of many untested drugs. Clearly, the employees of this agency are faced with difficult decisions that have important consequences for consumers.

False Advertising

Consumers depend on advertising to obtain information about goods and services. But some advertisements contain misleading information or outright lies. Often, the consumer is not in a position to evaluate the truth of advertising claims.

The Federal Trade Commission has the responsibility for detecting false advertising. When members of the commission become aware of a problem, they can order the firm to change its advertising.

In some cases, the commission has required a firm to advertise that it had been untruthful in the past. For example, one company claimed that its mouthwash would kill germs and protect users from the common cold. The Federal Trade Commission found that this was not true and ordered the company to advertise that, for cold protection, its mouthwash was no more effective than gargling with warm water.

GOVERNMENT AND WORKER PROTECTION

Government helps workers by making workplaces safer and by protecting workers from being treated unfairly while on the job.

Worker Safety

Certain occupations are known to be risky. Stunt riders and football players, for example, know that their jobs involve risk of injury. Their salaries reflect the dangers they face. Most workers, however, do not expect to suffer injury or illness on the job. They expect their employers to follow safety procedures and to provide safe working conditions.

Unfortunately, companies do not always operate safely, and every year thousands of people are injured on the job. Other people suffer serious health problems, such as cancer, because they are exposed to harmful chemicals in the workplace. In some cases, the harmful effects of these chemicals do not appear until long after the person has quit working in the plant.

Illus. 13-4 *Government regulations improve working conditions, but certain occupations, such as race car driving, still are very dangerous.*

The Occupational Safety and Health Administration is a federal agency established to maintain safety standards and improve working conditions. Employees of the agency inspect businesses to make sure that unsafe situations are corrected. A firm found to have safety problems can be fined, or, if the hazard is especially dangerous, it can be required to close until the problem is corrected.

Discrimination

Job opportunities and salaries in a free enterprise system should be determined by a worker's contribution to the business. Someone who is especially good at a job has the right to expect a promotion and more money than someone who cannot perform the tasks as well.

Unfortunately, job opportunities and pay sometimes depend on race, sex, age, or religion. When decisions are based on these factors rather than performance on the job, the employer is said to be practicing *discrimination*.

If just one employer discriminates against a class of workers, those workers may be able to find other jobs where they are treated more fairly. But if many employers practice discrimination, the workers may have difficulty finding good jobs.

There are laws against discrimination in the workplace. Firms that violate these laws can be fined by the government and sued by workers. Firms practicing discrimination may be prohibited from doing business with the government until they change their policies. Efforts by government have not eliminated discrimination in job markets, but they have made the practice less common.

Instant Replay

Because air and water are free, businesses have little incentive to preserve the environment. But government has the power to require firms to reduce their polluting.

Consumers are protected against unsafe products by agencies such as the National Highway Traffic Safety Administration, the Consumer Product Safety Commission, and the Food and Drug Administration.

The Federal Trade Commission is responsible for preventing false advertising. The Occupational Safety and Health Administration inspects working conditions to make sure that they are safe.

Firms that practice discrimination can be fined, sued, or prevented from doing business with the government.

GOVERNMENT AS A MANAGER OF THE ECONOMY

Important goals in any economic system are to reduce the rates of unemployment and inflation. This is the main reason the federal government collects information on unemployment and price changes. This information is useful in making decisions about how to improve economic performance in these areas. The methods used by the federal government in dealing with inflation and unemployment are rather complicated. However, the brief introduction presented in this section should help you understand the basic ideas.

As you know, demand-pull inflation results from too much money chasing too few goods and services. This suggests that one cure for inflation is to reduce the amount of money people have to spend. There are three ways this can be done. First, the

Federal Reserve System can reduce the supply of money. Second, the government can take money from individuals and businesses by raising taxes. Third, the government can reduce the demand for goods and services by cutting back on the amount of money it spends. All three of these methods can be used to deal with inflation. At different times, each has been used by the government.

Chapter 7 establishes that the demand for labor is a derived demand. This suggests that unemployment can be reduced if the demand for goods and services is increased. This can be accomplished using the same three tools suggested for cutting inflation. First, the supply of money could be increased. With more money, more goods and services would be demanded and more workers would be needed to produce them. Second, taxes could be cut. Again, with more money available for spending, the demand for goods and services would increase. This would mean more jobs. Finally, if the government buys more, job opportunities would be improved. Extra workers would be hired to produce these goods and services.

SUMMARY

Government acts as a referee in the economic system. The police and the courts protect individuals against theft and violence. The courts can require those who sign contracts to honor them. The courts also make decisions involving honest disagreements among individuals.

Banks use fractional reserve banking. This means that the banks keep only a small proportion of total deposits in their vaults. Fractional reserve banking works only as long as people have confidence in the banking system.

The Federal Reserve System was created to manage the money supply and to set banking policies. The Federal Reserve System provides currency to banks, acts as a clearinghouse for checks, holds reserves and makes loans to banks, and regulates the supply of money.

Government has a role in protecting the environment. Because air and water are free, businesses have little need to conserve these important natural resources. By setting standards, requiring pollution control devices, and using fines, government can force firms to reduce the amount of pollution they cause.

Government protects consumers by requiring that unsafe products be changed or removed from the market. It can also prevent companies from using false advertising. Various government agencies protect workers by requiring safety in the workplace and by enforcing laws against discrimination.

Reducing unemployment and inflation are two goals of government. Some methods to accomplish these objectives include changing tax rates, changing the supply of money, and changing the amount of goods and services purchased by government.

In the blank space, write the term that correctly completes the sentence.

1. The proportion of deposits that cannot be loaned out is called the _____.

2. The _____ is the central bank of the United States.

3. A _____ is a business that holds money deposited by others.

4. Every country has a _____ to supervise banking activities.

5. The practice of lending out part of the money deposited is called _____.

6. _____ are deposits that are not loaned out.

7. The _____ directs the activities of the Federal Reserve System.

8. When a worker's pay is determined by age, sex, or race, _____ is occurring.

REVIEW QUESTIONS

1. Give two examples of how government acts as a referee in the economic system.
2. Why does fractional reserve banking work only as long as people have confidence in the banking system?
3. What is the most important responsibility of the Federal Reserve System?
4. List three ways that government could reduce the rate of inflation.
5. What federal agency protects consumers against false advertising?
6. In a free enterprise system, why do firms often pollute the environment?
7. What type of workers frequently experience discrimination in the workplace?

14

Taxation

"The art of taxation consists of plucking the goose so as to obtain the largest amount of feathers with the least amount of hissing."

PREVIEW

Taxes are money that individuals and businesses are required to pay to the government. Taxes differ from other uses of money in that the taxpayer has no choice. You can choose whether to spend your income on a piano, motorcycle, or shotgun. But tax payments are not a matter of choice. The government can force you to pay taxes you owe.

About $1,500 billion in taxes are paid in the United States each year. This total represents approximately $1 out of every $3 earned. Most of these taxes go to the federal government. However, one-third of all tax dollars are paid to state and local governments.

This chapter will help you understand the tax system in the United States. When you have completed the reading and the learning activities, you should be able to:

- List four purposes of taxation.
- Explain the ability-to-pay and the benefits-received principles of taxation.
- Discuss the differences among progressive, proportional, and regressive taxes.
- Explain how the personal income tax, the social security tax, sales and excise taxes, and the property tax are used in the United States.
- Identify the most important sources of revenue for the federal government and for state and local governments.
- Identify the most important uses of money by the federal government and by state and local governments.

PURPOSES OF TAXATION

There are four main reasons that individuals and businesses are required to pay taxes. Taxation is used by the government to:
- Finance government activities
- Change consumer decisions
- Redistribute income
- Manage the economy

Finance Government Activities

The government, like a business, needs money to purchase goods and services and to pay its employees. The main purpose of taxation is to provide government with the income it needs to function. Taxes pay for tanks, missiles, and soldiers. They provide the money to build roads, dams, and bridges. They pay school teachers, finance building construction, and buy fire engines. Tax money is also used to help poor countries, to explore space, and to provide medical care.

Change Consumer Decisions

Taxes can be used to change consumer decisions. Sometimes a government's objective is to reduce consumption of a good or service. For example, faced with congested roads and the need to buy large quantities of oil from other nations, the leaders of many European countries decided to reduce gasoline consumption by making use of the law of demand. They imposed high taxes on gasoline to make it much more expensive and to cause people to cut back on their driving.

Cigarettes and alcohol are other examples of goods that are heavily taxed. These taxes help finance the activities of government, and they discourage the use of these products by increasing their prices.

Redistribute Income

In the United States some people are rich, but many others are poor. By imposing heavier taxes on the wealthy, the government can use taxes to equalize the distribution of income. Some of the tax money collected may be used to assist low-income groups.

Manage the Economy

Taxes are used as a tool for managing the economy. Changing the amount of taxes paid by individuals and businesses may increase the number of jobs, reduce the inflation rate, and increase the rate

U.S. Department of Energy

Illus. 14-1 *Taxes provide the government with money it needs to build and maintain dams.*

of growth of GNP. This use of the money collected by taxes is discussed in Chapter 13.

PRINCIPLES OF TAXATION

There are many different types of taxes. How should elected government officials decide what types and amounts of taxes should be paid by each individual and business? These are difficult questions. However, there are two basic principles that can be used as a guide:

- Ability to pay
- Benefits received

Ability to Pay

Consider the following situation. Allen Jackson earns $10,000 each year. Juan Garcia has an income of $100,000 per year. Suppose the tax system requires each to pay $5,000 in taxes. Which person will find the tax payment the most difficult? For Juan Garcia, paying the tax might mean that he will vacation in Hawaii instead of taking a round-the-world trip. For Allen Jackson, coming up with $5,000 could mean there is no money left for rent and clothes.

The *ability-to-pay* principle bases the amount of taxes on the ability to pay those taxes. This means that those with high incomes should usually be asked to pay more taxes than those with low incomes. In the United States, the personal income tax is based on the ability-to-pay principle. More information about the personal income tax is presented later in this chapter.

Benefits Received

In a free enterprise system, the goods and services that people receive depend on the amount of money they spend. If you want to drive a new Porsche, you must pay the price of a new Porsche. To travel first-class on an airplane, you must be willing to spend extra dollars for a first-class ticket.

The *benefits-received* principle of taxation relates the amount of taxes paid to services received. Those who benefit most are those who should pay the most taxes.

The tax on gasoline is an example of benefits-received taxation. The dollars collected from this tax are used to build and improve roads. The more a person drives, the more benefits she or he receives from having a good road system. However, because more driving requires more gasoline, the amount of gas tax paid increases with the amount of driving. Thus, those who benefit the most are those who pay the most.

Illus. 14-2 *An example of benefits-received taxation is the tax on gasoline which is used to build and improve roads.*

The Asphalt Institute

Taxes are payments that individuals and businesses are required to make to the government.

Taxes are used to (1) finance government activities, (2) change consumer decisions, (3) redistribute income, and (4) manage the economy.

The ability-to-pay principle of taxation suggests that taxes should be based on the capacity of people to pay. The benefits-received principle ties tax payments to the benefits obtained from government.

PROGRESSIVE, PROPORTIONAL, AND REGRESSIVE TAXES

The total amount of money paid as taxes is determined by the tax base and the tax rate. The **tax base** is the number of dollars to be taxed. The **tax rate** is the proportion of each dollar in the tax base that must be paid as taxes.

For example, consider a tax on the amount of money earned by a person. Such a tax is called a personal income tax. Suppose the tax applies to $20,000 in income. This is the tax base. Also suppose that 20 percent of each dollar of income is to be paid as tax. Twenty percent is the tax rate. The total tax is determined by multiplying the tax base by the tax rate. In the example, the tax would be 20 percent of $20,000, or $4,000.

Progressive Taxes

The tax rate may change at different levels of income. The proportion of extra dollars that must be paid as taxes is called the **marginal tax rate**. Suppose the marginal tax rates for an income tax are as shown in Table 14-1. The table indicates a rate of 10 percent of the first $10,000 in income earned. For income between $10,000 and $20,000, the rate is 20 percent. For all income above $20,000, the rate is 30 percent.

Using the rates from Table 14-1, how much tax would be paid by someone with an income of $40,000? Ten percent of the first

$10,000 would be $1,000. Twenty percent of the next $10,000 would be $2,000. The 30 percent rate would apply to the final $20,000 of earnings and would total $6,000. Thus, the total tax is $1,000 plus $2,000 plus $6,000, or $9,000.

Table 14-1 *This table illustrates how a progressive tax works.*

Progressive Tax

Income	Marginal Tax Rate
$0–10,000	10%
10,001–20,000	20%
20,001 and above	30%

Table 14-1 illustrates a **progressive tax**. A progressive tax has increasing marginal tax rates. This means people pay a higher proportion of extra dollars of income in taxes as their incomes increase. In Table 14-1, the marginal tax rate is increasing. It goes from 10 percent on the first dollars earned to 30 percent on dollars earned beyond $20,000.

Progressive taxes are based on the ability-to-pay principle of taxation. The principle is that those with higher incomes are more able to pay taxes. Thus, the proportion of high-income dollars taken by the tax is greater than the proportion of low-income dollars. The personal income tax is an example of a progressive tax.

Proportional Taxes

If the percentage of income paid to taxes is the same at all levels of income, the tax is called a **proportional tax**. An income tax with a constant marginal rate of 20 percent would be an example of a proportional tax because people at all income levels would pay 20 percent of their income as taxes.

Regressive Taxes

A **regressive tax** has decreasing marginal tax rates. Table 14-2 is an example of a regressive tax. The tax is 10 percent on the first $10,000 in income. The next $10,000 is taxed at 5 percent. On all additional dollars of income the tax is 2 percent.

Regressive taxes do not follow the ability-to-pay principle. High-income dollars are not taxed as heavily as low-income dollars. A regressive tax may be unfair to low-income groups. Thus, a good tax system should avoid regressive taxes.

Economics of Work

Table 14-2 *This table illustrates how a regressive tax works.*

Regressive Tax

Income	Marginal Tax Rate
$0–10,000	10%
10,001–20,000	5%
20,001 and above	2%

Instant Replay

Progressive taxes are based on the idea that those with higher incomes are able to pay more taxes. Such taxes use increasing marginal tax rates.

With proportional taxes, the percentage of income paid as taxes is the same for all income levels.

Regressive taxes have decreasing marginal tax rates. They may impose a heavy burden on low-income groups.

TYPES OF TAXES

Dozens of different taxes are used in the United States. There is a tax on money that is inherited. There is a tax on gifts. Profits of corporations are taxed. Some states place a special tax on the use of hotel rooms. Other states tax coal and oil taken from the ground. The government also taxes companies that pollute the environment. However, there are four types of taxes you are most likely to pay:

- Personal income tax
- Social security tax
- Sales and excise taxes
- Property tax

Personal Income Tax

The *personal income tax* is a tax on the income of individuals. Taxes such as the personal income tax that are levied on people are called *direct taxes*. The federal government uses a personal income tax. So do many states and some cities. Because the tax laws of the states and cities are so different, only the federal personal income tax is discussed here.

Illus. 14-3 *Working students are likely to pay little personal income tax because their total earnings are low.*

The federal personal income tax is a progressive tax. Thus, the marginal tax rate for high incomes is greater than at lower levels of income. Table 14-3 shows the tax rates set by Congress for 1988. Note that the first column is labeled *taxable income*. This is the tax base to which the tax rates are applied. A person's taxable income is not the same as the total amount of money earned. In determining your income tax, you are allowed to subtract certain types of expenses. These include interest payments, money given to charity, medical bills, and some other items. Taxable income is also affected by the number of people in the family. Under current laws, taxable income is reduced by about $2,000 for each person in the family.

Table 14-3 *This table gives the personal income tax rate for 1988 for a married couple.*

Federal Personal Income Tax Rate: 1988*

Taxable Income	Marginal Tax Rate
$0–29,750	15%
above 29,750	28%

*Married couple filing jointly

Table 14-3 shows that the marginal tax rate increases as income rises. For a married couple, the marginal tax rate is 15 percent for the first $29,750 in taxable income and 28 percent of each additional dollar of income.

198

The actual amount of taxes paid is usually less than the amounts that would be calculated from Table 14-3. There are two reasons. The first is *tax loopholes*. Loopholes are legal ways of reducing the amount of income tax owed. Hundreds of different loopholes are written into the tax laws. The second method is tax evasion. *Tax evasion* means cheating on income tax payments. The most common method is by not listing all the income that was earned during the year. Tax evasion is becoming an important problem in the United States. It is estimated that the government loses about $90 billion each year because of tax cheating.

Tax forms must be filed by April 15 of each year. However, if all taxes were paid at once, the federal government would be short of money much of the time. The solution is *tax withholding*. Withholding means that employers automatically take out, or withhold, part of their employees' salaries. This money is then sent to the federal government. Employers use tables provided by the government to determine the amount to withhold. Sometimes, the amount withheld is different from the total taxes owed by the person for the year. If too much money has been withheld, then the taxpayer can get a refund from the government. If too little has been withheld, additional taxes must be paid.

Social Security Tax

In 1935, Congress passed the Federal Insurance Contribution Act (FICA). Its purpose was to provide income and medical assistance for the elderly and other persons unable to care for their own needs.

Under this system, employed persons pay *social security* taxes during their working years. These taxes are collected by employers, who deduct the money from employee paychecks. The employer also matches the amount paid by the employee. For self-employed workers, the total tax is paid by the individual.

The social security taxes collected go into a special fund. Workers who retire or become disabled are given monthly payments to replace a part of their lost income. The family of a worker who dies can also receive money from this fund.

Sales and Excise Taxes

Sales and excise taxes are taxes on the purchase of goods and services. Taxes levied on things instead of people are called *indirect taxes*. A *sales tax* usually applies to almost all of the things a consumer purchases. In contrast, an *excise tax* is a tax on the purchase of a specific good or service.

Illus. 14-4 *One purpose of the social security system is to provide some income for retired people who may have difficulty caring for their own needs.*

The federal government does not use a general sales tax, but most of the states do. The state sales tax is a percentage of the selling price of the item. In states where it is used, the sales tax varies from 2 percent to 7 percent.

Excise taxes are used by both the federal government and the state governments. Items covered include alcoholic beverages, tobacco, gasoline, tires, movies, and airline tickets.

Property Tax

State and local governments have used the property tax for many years. There are two types of property tax. A *real property tax* is a tax on land, buildings, and other things that cannot be easily moved. A *personal property tax* applies to cars, boats, airplanes, and other easily movable possessions.

Both types of property tax are computed in the same way. The *assessed value* of the property is determined first. In some cases, this could be the actual value of the property. But usually it is less than the actual value. For example, in many states the assessed value is only about 20 percent of actual value. The assessed value is the tax base of the property tax. The tax is computed by multiplying the assessed value by the tax rate.

Instant Replay

The federal personal income tax is a direct tax. It is also a progressive tax.

The social security tax is collected from workers to provide income for retired persons and others who are unable to meet their own financial needs.

A sales tax usually applies to almost all the goods and services that a consumer purchases. Excise taxes apply to specific purchases.

The property tax is a tax on land, buildings, and other kinds of property.

SOURCES OF GOVERNMENT REVENUE

Figure 14-1 shows the most important sources of revenue for the federal government. Revenue includes taxes and all other money received. The personal income tax is the main source. Almost one-half of all money received comes from this tax. The corporation income tax is a tax on the profits of corporations. This source provides about 10 cents out of every federal revenue dollar.

Figure 14-2 indicates where the money comes from to support state and local governments. The most important sources shown are sales, excise, and property taxes. Another important source of income for state and local governments is dollars received from the federal government. The contribution of income taxes is much less than for the federal government.

USES OF GOVERNMENT REVENUE

In a recent year the federal government spent a total of $994 billion ($994,000,000,000). It is difficult to comprehend such a large number, but you can understand it better if you look at the following comparisons. If you had $994 billion you could:
•Spend $1 million a day for over 2,000 years.

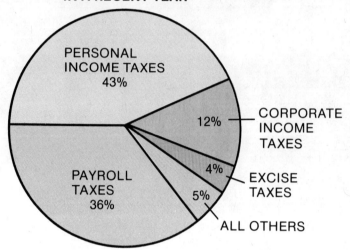

SOURCES OF FEDERAL REVENUE IN A RECENT YEAR

PERSONAL INCOME TAXES 43%

CORPORATE INCOME TAXES 12%

EXCISE TAXES 4%

ALL OTHERS 5%

PAYROLL TAXES 36%

Figure 14-1 *This illustration shows the sources from which the federal government receives revenue.*

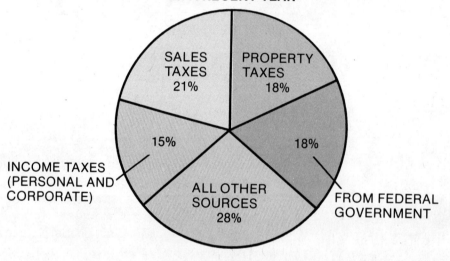

SOURCES OF STATE AND LOCAL REVENUE IN A RECENT YEAR

SALES TAXES 21%

PROPERTY TAXES 18%

INCOME TAXES (PERSONAL AND CORPORATE) 15%

ALL OTHER SOURCES 28%

FROM FEDERAL GOVERNMENT 18%

Figure 14-2 *This illustration shows the sources from which state and local governments receive their revenues.*

- Buy a new Cadillac for everyone in the state of Texas.
- Make a path of dollar bills nearly 600 feet wide that would encircle the earth at its equator.

Table 14-4 shows how the federal government spends its money. The largest single category is income security. This category includes all the federal government's programs to provide a minimum income to unemployed, disabled, and retired people. Most of this money goes out in social security payments, but payments include unemployment compensation and welfare

202

benefits as well. About 30 percent of total expenditures are used for national defense. Interest is nearly 15 percent of the total and represents payments to those who have lent money to the federal government.

Table 14-4 *Uses of federal government dollars in a recent year.*

Federal Government Expenditures

Category	Percentage of Total Expenditures
Income Security	39.9%
National Defense	28.4
Interest	14.9
Health	3.5
Education and Employment	2.8
Veterans' Benefits	2.7
Transportation	2.6
Natural Resources	1.2
Other	4.0

Illus. 14-5 *28.4% of the federal government's expenditures is used for defense.*

U.S. Department of the Navy

State and local governments spend about one-half the amount spent by the federal government. Table 14-5 shows how these dollars were used. The spending pattern is much different from that of the federal government. State and local governments spend the largest part of their money on education, highways, and public welfare (such as money for hospitals and assistance to the poor).

Table 14-5 *Uses of state and local government dollars in a recent year.*

State and Local Government Expenditures

Category	Percentage of Total Expenditures
Education	34.9%
Public Welfare	13.2
Highways	7.8
Other	44.1

Instant Replay

The income tax is the most important source of revenue for the federal government.

State and local governments rely heavily on the property tax and on sales and excise taxes. A part of their revenue comes from the federal government.

Income security and national defense are the two most important uses of money at the federal level.

Education is the largest use of money at the state and local level.

SUMMARY

Taxes are payments that individuals and businesses are required to make to the government. They are used to finance government activities, to redistribute income, to change consumer decisions, and to manage the economy.

The ability-to-pay principle of taxation suggests that high-income groups should be taxed more heavily than low-income people. The benefits-received principle implies that those who receive the most benefits should pay the most taxes.

The marginal tax rate is the proportion of extra dollars due as the tax base increases. Progressive taxes have increasing marginal tax rates, while regressive taxes have decreasing marginal tax rates. With a proportional tax, people at all income levels pay the same percent of income as taxes.

The federal personal income tax is a progressive tax. Tax withholding is used to provide the government with a year-round flow of revenue.

The social security tax is used to provide assistance to those who have difficulty caring for their own needs. Sales and excise taxes are taxes on the purchase of goods and services. Property taxes are paid on buildings and land and on items such as cars and boats.

The most important source of revenue for the federal government is the personal income tax. Sources of support at the state and local levels include sales, excise, and property taxes. In addition, state and local governments receive money from the federal government.

Over half of federal expenditures are for national defense and social security payments. The most important uses of money at the state and local levels are for education, highways, and hospitals.

BUILDING YOUR VOCABULARY

proportional tax
ability to pay
benefits received
tax base
tax rate
personal income tax
marginal tax rate
progressive tax
regressive taxes
taxable income
tax loophole
tax evasion
tax withholding
social security
sales tax
excise tax
real property
personal property
assessed value
direct taxes
indirect tax taxes

In the blank space, write the term that correctly completes the sentence.

1. Taxes with decreasing marginal rates are called _____.

2. The proportion of extra dollars paid in taxes is the _____.

3. The number of dollars taxed is the _____.

4. With a _____ the percentage of income paid as taxes stays the same regardless of income.

5. The _____ system provides income for retired persons and those unable to care for themselves.

6. A _____ is a tax on almost all goods and services purchased.

7. The practice of deducting income taxes from an employee's paycheck is called _____.

8. A tax on a specific good or service is an _____.

9. A tax with increasing marginal tax rates is a _____.

10. _____ are money that must be paid to the government.

11. A progressive tax is an example of _____ taxation.

12. _____ are levied on people.

13. The percentage of income going to taxes is the _____.

14. The _____ is based on the income earned by individuals.

15. The value of property for tax purposes is called _____.

16. Illegal avoidance of taxes is called _____.

17. A legal way of reducing taxes is by using a _____.

18. Land and buildings are examples of _____.

19. A car is an example of _____.

20. An _____ is levied on things.

21. A tax on gasoline is an example of taxing based on the _____ principle.

22. Income subject to taxes is _____.

REVIEW QUESTIONS

1. How can taxes be used to change the goods and services purchased by consumers?
2. What is the ability-to-pay principle of taxation?
3. Give an example of a progressive tax.
4. Why is taxable income usually less than total dollars earned?
5. Why does the federal government use tax withholding?
6. What is the purpose of the social security tax?
7. What is the difference between a sales tax and an excise tax?
8. What is the most important source of revenue for the federal government?

GLOSSARY

ability to pay A principle of fair taxation based on a person's capacity to pay taxes.

absolute advantage The ability of one country to produce a product at a lower cost than another nation.

advertising Actions by a business to make consumers aware of its product and to persuade them to buy it.

AFL-CIO The national organization that represents organized labor in political lobbying and public relations.

agent A person or firm that has been given the right to act for others.

assembly line A device that moves a product from one worker to the next as it is being manufactured.

assessed value The tax base of the property tax.

asset Something owned by or owed to a person or business.

automation The replacement of human labor by machines.

balance of trade The difference between money received from exports and money spent on imports.

bank A business that keeps money deposited by individuals and businesses.

barter The exchange of goods and services without the use of money.

benefits received A principle of fair taxation based on the services a person receives from government.

board of directors The governing body of a corporation.

Board of Governors of the Federal Reserve System A group that consists of seven members with overall responsibility for administering the Federal Reserve System.

bond A printed promise to repay a certain amount of money, at a certain interest rate, at a certain time.

business cycle Alternating periods of increase and decrease in gross national product.

capital gain An increase in the value of shares of stock.

capital goods Goods that are used to produce other goods.

capitalist economy An economic system where individuals are allowed to own capital goods.

central bank An organization responsible for all banking in a country.

channel of distribution The path that goods take as they move from the original producer to the final customer.

charter A document that gives a business legal authority to operate.

checkbook money Dollars that people have in their checking accounts.

circular flow of income The continuous movement of income between product and resource markets.

closed shop A place of business that hires only union members.

coins Money made of metal.

command system An economic system in which decisions are made by government or a small group of people.

communist society A form of socialist economy.

comparative advantage The ability of one country to produce a product relatively more efficiently than another nation.

competition Attempts by business to attract customers and factors of production.

consumer goods Goods purchased by consumers.

Consumer Price Index A measure of the change in prices of goods and services used by most people.

consumers People who buy goods and services.

consumption The final use of goods and services.

contract A legal agreement between two or more people to do or not to do something.

cooperative A business owned by the people who use its services.

corporation A business owned by several persons, each of whom has limited liability.

cost-push inflation An increase in prices resulting from increases in the cost of production.

craft union A labor union consisting of workers with a particular skill.

credit An agreement to buy something today and pay for it later.

creditor Someone who is owed money.

currency Paper money.

debtor One who owes money.

deflation A general decrease in the prices of a market basket of goods.

demand The amount of a good or service that people are willing and able to buy at a specific price.

demand curve A graph showing the relationship between price and quantity demanded.

demand-pull inflation An increase in prices resulting from too much money chasing too few goods.

depression A period when Real GNP is falling very rapidly and the number of people without jobs is large.

derived demand The demand for factors of production that is dependent on the demand for the product made by the factors of production.

direct tax A tax levied on people.

discrimination The practice of paying some workers less than others for the same job.

distribution of income The manner in which income is divided between people.

dividends The portion of a corporation's profits set aside for payment to stockholders.

economics The study of the use of scarce resources.

economic system The organizations, laws, traditions, beliefs, and habits that affect decision making in a society.

economies of scale Lower costs resulting from large-scale production.

economy The system used in a nation for making decisions on what, how, and for whom to produce.

elastic demand A situation where a small change in price results in a large change in quantity demanded.

employee A person who works for someone else.

entrepreneurs Persons in a free enterprise system who organize the factors of production and are willing to take risks to earn profits.

environment The water, air, vegetation, and other surroundings in an area.

excess demand A situation in which more is demanded than is supplied.

excess supply A situation in which more is supplied than is demanded.

excise tax A tax on a specific item that is purchased.

expansion A phase of the business cycle during which GNP is increasing.

exports Goods sold to other countries.

factors of production Human, natural, and capital resources used to produce goods and services.

Federal Reserve System The central banking system of the United States.

firm Another name for a business.

fractional reserve banking The practice of lending out much of the money that has been deposited in a bank.

franchise The legal right to sell a company's product or service in a specific area.

free enterprise system An economic system in which households and managers of firms are free to make their own earning and spending decisions.

fringe benefits Payments to workers in addition to the wages or salaries that they receive.

full employment An unemployment rate of about 5 or 6 percent.

goods Objects of value that can be measured or weighed.

grievance procedure A way of settling disagreements between employers and workers.

Gross National Product (GNP) The dollar value of all final goods and services produced in the economy.

household A small group of people who make their earning and spending decisions together.

human resources The efforts and skills that individuals contribute to producing goods and services.

imports Goods purchased from other countries.

income The reward received from the sale of resources.

indirect tax A tax levied on things.

Industrial Revolution The period when machines were first widely used to increase efficiency and cut costs in manufacturing.

industrial union A labor union that includes all the workers in an industry.

industry All of the firms that make a particular product.

inelastic demand A situation where even a large change in price causes only a small change in quantity demanded.

inflation An increase in the price of a market basket of goods and services.

interdependence The reliance of workers and businesses on one another.

interest rate The price charged for the use of money.

intermediary A person or business whose job is to bring buyers and sellers together.

international trade The exchange of goods and services produced in different countries.

labor union A group of workers who have joined together to improve their wages and working conditions.

law of demand A principle stating that people tend to buy more of something at lower prices than they do at higher prices.

law of diminishing returns A situation where extra workers do not add as much extra output as those already hired.

law of supply A principle stating that firms will produce more of a good at higher prices than they will at lower prices.

limited liability A situation where a business owner cannot lose more than he/she invested in the business.

marginal cost The extra cost of producing one more unit of output.

marginal tax rate The proportion of extra dollars of income that must be paid as taxes.

market An arrangement that allows buyers and sellers to come together to exchange goods, services, and resources.

market basket A set of goods and services purchased by the typical family.

market price The price at which supply and demand are equal.

market wage The wage at which labor supply and demand are equal.

marketing The connecting link between producers and consumers.

market power A situation where a business has only a limited need to compete.

mass production The production of goods and services in large quantities using specialization of labor.

medium of exchange Something which is generally accepted in trade.

mixed system An economic system in which most decisions are left to individuals, but some decisions are made by government.

money Anything that people are willing to accept as payment for things they sell or for work they do.

monopoly A firm that is the single seller of a good or service.

multiplied effect A total increase in employment greater than the number of jobs created by a new business.

National Labor Relations Act A law that gave unions a legal right to exist and required employers to negotiate contracts with union representatives.

natural resources Materials that come from the air, water, and earth.

needs Goods and services that people must have to continue living.

oligopoly A market that consists of a small number of sellers.

opportunity cost The value of resources in their best alternative use.

partnership A business owned by two or more people.

peak The top of the business cycle.

Per Capita Income Total income divided by the number of people.

personal income tax A tax on income earned by an individual.

personal property tax A tax on cars, boats, and other personal property.

picket line A group of workers marching in front of a business to call attention to their demands.

private enterprise system An economic system in which people make decisions as private individuals rather than as part of a public or government group.

private property Property owned by individuals.

profit motive The desire to earn profits.

profits The dollars left over after a business has paid all of its expenses.

progressive tax A tax with an increasing marginal tax rate.

property tax A tax on land, buildings, and vehicles.

proportional tax A tax such that the percentage of income paid as taxes is the same regardless of income.

rate of unemployment The percentage of the work force without a job.

Real Gross National Product (Real GNP) Gross national product adjusted for changes in prices.

real property tax A tax on land and buildings.

recession A period during which Real GNP declines.

regressive tax A tax with decreasing marginal tax rates.

rent The payment received for the use of land and/or buildings.

reserve ratio The portion of total deposits that cannot be loaned out by a bank.

reserves Bank funds kept on hand to meet the everyday withdrawal needs of depositors.

resource markets Markets where human, natural, and capital resources are exchanged.

retailer A business that buys goods to sell them to consumers.

right-to-work law A state law that outlaws the union shop.

salary A regular income paid for work over a set time period.

sales tax A tax on almost all things purchased.

scarcity A condition in which more goods and services are desired than are available.

service Help received from other people.

share One unit of ownership in a corporation.

socialist economy An economic system where the government owns the means of production.

social security tax A tax that employed persons pay during their working years to provide income for retired people and for those unable to care for themselves.

society A group of individuals who have similar goals or interests.

sole proprietorship A business owned by only one person.

specialization of labor The assignment of workers to specific tasks.

stockbrokers Those people who assist investors in buying and selling stocks.

stock certificate A document showing ownership in a corporation.

stock exchange A place where shares of stock are bought and sold.

stockholders The owners of a corporation.

store of value Something that can be held to buy goods or services in the future.

strike An agreement by workers to stop working.

supply The quantity of a good or service that firms will provide at different prices.

supply curve A graph showing the amount that firms will supply at different prices.

Taft–Hartley Act A law that limits the power of unions and allows the President of the United States to delay a strike.

tariff A tax on imported goods.

taxable income That portion of total income which is taxed.

tax base The number of dollars to be taxed.

tax evasion Illegal avoidance of taxes.

tax loopholes Legal methods of reducing taxes.

tax rate The proportion of each dollar in the tax base that must be paid as taxes.

tax withholding The practice of deducting income taxes from an employee's paycheck.

taxes Money that must be paid to the government.

trade The exchange of goods, services, and resources.

trough The bottom of the business cycle.

union shop A place of business in which new workers must join a union within a short time after starting work.

unit of account The means by which prices are expressed.

utility The ability of goods and services to satisfy human needs and wants.

wage Compensation that depends on the amount of time worked.

wage-price spiral Wages pushing prices up, which in turn push wages up further.

wants Desires for goods or services that people could live without but that make life more pleasant.

wholesaler A business that buys goods from producers and then sells them to retailers.

INDEX

Page numbers in *italics* refer to figures in the text.

Firm, defined, 2
Form utility, 139
Fractional reserve banking, defined, 179
Franchise, defined, 84
Freedom of choice: and economic systems, 3; in command system, 5; in free enterprise system, 3; in mixed system, 7
Free enterprise systems: defined, 3; freedom to buy in, 3; freedom to own property in, 3; freedom to produce and sell in, 4; freedom to work in, 4
Fringe benefits, as goal of labor unions, 109
Full employment, 169

GNP. See Gross National Product
Goods: defined, 13; demand for, 50; the supply of, 46. See also Capital resources
Government: activities financed by taxation, 192; and consumer protection, 184; and environmental protection, 183; and worker protection, 186; as a banker, 179; as a manager of the economy, 188; as a referee in economic system, 177; expenditures of federal, 203; expenditures of state, and local, 204
Government assistance, as a cause of market power, 69
Government regulations, laws affecting labor unions, 105
Government revenue: sources of, 201; sources of federal, 202; sources of state and local, 202; uses of, 201
Grading of products, 133
Grievance procedures, 110
Gross National Product: and per capita income, 165; defined, 166; Real, 167

Health, and human resources, 16
Household, defined, 2
Household workers, job prospects for, 94
Human resources, defined, 14
Human wants, unlimited, 12

Imports, defined, 151
Income: circular flow of, 29; distribution of, 98, 99; Gross National Product and, 164; markets and, 28; Per Capita, 167; redistributed by taxation, 192; sources of, 95, 98
Income tax: as a source of federal, state, and local revenue, 202; personal, 197; rates for 1988, 198
Industrial Revolution, 103
Industrial union, 104. See also labor unions
Industry, defined, 2
Inelastic demand, defined, 53
Inflation: causes of, 162; defined,

160; demand-pull, 163; gainers and losers from, 160; measuring the rate of, 164; rate from 1970 to 1987, 165
Interdependence, defined, 127
Interest, as a source of income, 98
Interest rate(s): and investment in capital goods, 117; defined, 98, 116; and the demand for capital goods, 119
Intermediaries, defined, 135
International trade: advantages of, 152; defined, 148; disadvantages of, 153
Investment in capital goods, 116; interest rates and, 117

Job losses, risk of, and business closings, 146
Job opportunities. See Employment opportunities
Jobs, the demand for, 90
Job security, as goal of labor unions, 110

Labor: derived demand for, 90; downward-sloping, demand curves, 91; specialization of, 124
Labor unions: AFL-CIO, 104; craft, 104; defined, 103; fringe benefits, 109; goals of, 108; grievance procedures, 110; history, 103; in action, 110; independent, 106; industrial, 104; job security, 110; laws affecting, 105; local, 108; national, 108; organization in the United States, 106; wages, 109; working conditions, 110; working hours, 109
Law of demand, defined, 51. See also Demand, Demand curves
Law of diminishing returns, 92
Law of supply, defined, 48. See also Supply, Supply curves
Laws, affecting labor unions, 105
Limited liability, defined, 77
Limited resources, 17
Local unions, 108. See also Labor unions

Managers, job prospects, 93
Marginal cost, defined, 48
Marginal tax rate, 195
Market(s): and the circular flow of income, 28; at work, 27; defined, 27; product, 28; resource, 28; the need for, 27; what, how, and for whom to produce, 30
Market basket, 164
Market economy, importance of money in a, 33
Marketing: and the utility of goods and services, 139; defined, 130; importance of, 131
Marketing functions, 132; buying, 132; financing, 134; grading and standardizing, 133; risk-taking, 134; selling, 134; storing, 133; transporting, 134
Market power: advertising effects

and, 69; causes of, 68; defined, 67; economies of scale and, 68; government assistance and, 69; problems created by, 70; resource control and, 68; superior skill and, 68
Market price: defined, 55; supply, demand, and, 53
Market wage, defined, 97
Mass production, defined, 125
Medium of exchange, defined, 5
Mixed systems, 7; defined, 8
Money: as a medium of exchange, 35; availability of, 37; as a store of value, 36; as a unit of account, 35; checkbook, 38; coins, 38; currency, 38; divisibility of, 38; durability of, 38; importance of, in a market economy, 33; responsibility of Federal Reserve System to regulate the supply of, 183; three functions of, 35; types of, 38; uniqueness of, 38; what makes "good," 36
Monopoly, defined, 70
Multiplied effect, 144

National Labor Relations Act, 105
National unions, organization of, 108. See also Labor unions
Natural resources, defined, 16
Needs: defined, 12; vs. wants, 12
Nonfarm laborers, job prospects for, 94

Occupational Outlook Handbook, 95
Oligopoly, defined, 71
Operatives, job prospects for, 94
Opportunity costs: and choices, 20; defined, 21; prices and, 43
Ownership, forms of retail stores, 136
Owning a business, 75

Partnerships, 79; advantages of, 80; as a percent of total businesses in U.S., 83; defined, 76; disadvantages of, 80; sales, as a percent of total businesses in U.S., 83
Peak, as part of business cycle, 171
Per Capita Income, defined, 167
Personal income tax, 197; rate for 1988, 198
Personal property tax, 200
Picket lines, 111
Place utility, 139
Possession utility, 140
Price(s): and opportunity costs, 43; as signals, 44; market, 55; supply, demand, and the market, 53; the importance of, 43; what, how, and for whom to produce and, 45. See also Market price
Price competition, 64
Private property, defined, 3
Produce, freedom to, 4
Producers, and channel of distribution, 137